Soliloquy
of a
SMALL-TOWN UNCIVIL
SERVANT

K.K. Srivastava is Director General in the office of Comptroller & Auditor General of India, New Delhi. A reticent and reclusive person, he has earned wide recognition in literary circles with his three volumes of poetry: *Ineluctable Stillness* (2005); *An Armless Hand Writes* (2008; 2012) and *Shadows of the Real* (2012). He is literary reviewer and columnist for the newspapers *The Pioneer* and *The Daily Star*.

Soliloquy
~of a~
SMALL-TOWN UNCIVIL SERVANT

K.K. SRIVASTAVA

RUPA

Published by
Rupa Publications India Pvt. Ltd 2019
7/16, Ansari Road, Daryaganj
New Delhi 110002

Sales centres:
Allahabad Bengaluru Chennai
Hyderabad Jaipur Kathmandu
Kolkata Mumbai

Copyright © K.K. Srivastava 2019

The views and opinions expressed in this book are the author's own and the facts are as reported by him which have been verified to the extent possible, and the publishers are not in any way liable for the same.

All rights reserved.
No part of this publication may be reproduced, transmitted, or stored in a retrieval system, in any form or by any means, electronic, mechanical, photocopying, recording or otherwise, without the prior permission of the publisher.

ISBN: 978-93-5304-083-3

First impression 2019

10 9 8 7 6 5 4 3 2 1

The moral right of the author has been asserted.

Printed by Nutech Print Services, Faridabad

This book is sold subject to the condition that it shall not, by way of trade or otherwise, be lent, resold, hired out, or otherwise circulated, without the publisher's prior consent, in any form of binding or cover other than that in which it is published.

*We are huge figures at small doors,
of caves looking into the blue...(blur),*

...

*we rub selves against what is not there,
and we laugh and cry out.*

Michael McClure

*An indispensable anodyne but for which
I could not have written this book.*

Contents

A *Prologue*	ix
1. Growing Up in Gorakhpur	1
2. Early Adolescence: Professor Yadav and My Uncle	14
3. Rendezvous With a New World	33
4. The Dream and Suicide	45
5. On Sex and Sensuality	51
6. The Behemothic Ethos	84
7. The Psychiatrist and Awareness	100
8. Within the Cave or the Cave Within	107
9. Authors, Books and Human Behaviour Chronicled	120
10. Of Social Niceties	143
11. Women of Literature and Women in Literature	162
12. A Half-made Place and Its People	177
13. Of Social Media	188
14. Time to Say Adieu	195

A Prologue

Very early morning, when night has started covering its visage and day lifting its veil, I wake up to find I have lost all my memories. Everything important or unimportant to me has been lost: my childhood, my parents, transitioning from school to college, then university, teachers, friends, my kin, Professor Yadav, a bachelor uncle, books read, words written, my six-and-a-half feet tall red jacket-wearing friend, unloved beloveds—all forgotten. Tabula rasa. I have to retrieve afresh. A new blackboard stares directly into my eyes. No chalks around. It is going to be a terrifying experience but I must undertake this journey in order to unravel the story that will discover me. That, of course, will not be the only discovery. Through periods of perplexity, of quietude and finally introspection, I will reach the core of the disjointed identities. There is no shunning it or shying away from it—this reaching. I have to face it.

As is the case with any writer, I will indulge in bringing the readers close to my reality, a world which might not get reflected in theirs. Readers, remember though, that this is not a memoir; it is at the most semi-autobiographical and that too, in parts. What is going to be set out will be in the nature of restoration: I will be enveloping it into a form that restores me to myself. A fugacious canvas spread out where movements are not to be restricted; each day's memories represent that day's highlights.

Naked curiosity is my greatest weapon and the weaving and unweaving of this curiosity, my wisest strength. What should I name it? Or let it be nameless. No, it's a soliloquy: I, in conversation with myself. An interior monologue. Experience of a fragmentary world or a phantasmagoric world, on the surface, where one moment leads me to another—so different and at such variance with the preceding one? Fragments animate associations—all kinds—between moments, images, mirages, conflicts, cadences, intonations, feelings and above all, human beings. These associations bring out in me the writer. In order to look back, a writer needs to access a pathway or many by walking on which he comes closer to those ambivalent associations which have stayed quiescent and continue to do so.

∽

I got the first glimpse of the capability in me to write in 1988 when I wrote my first poem titled, 'Birth Trauma'—a poem about the trauma of birth, comparing a mother's womb to the Stygian pool. This poem laid the foundations for a journey I was to take as a writer as I grew.

As I recall how I grew up amidst the unevolved planes of a place called Gorakhpur, a small district or better call it a town, in eastern Uttar Pradesh, I am reminded of being born not to an extraordinary fate but the one that befits those who are ill-fated. It was a society inhibited by people with no inclination to see outside of themselves. Thus I had no choice but to grow amidst bleary faces given to living in a state of denial and vacuity. Overcoming the general dogged determination to succumb to dictates of such a society, I delve back to a past which has its own awkwardness; as said before, it is an onerous journey not without pain. Was I not a subject matter of nightmarish childhood marked by unassuageable anxiety, resurfacing in the form of relentlessly dark, squeezing dreams and traumas? The creature ascended the monoliths but I never hid myself. As my travails as a writer began, I was aware of the sentient pain accompanying it. The travails introduce me to vast fields acting as sequesters when I make an incursion. I know of the impeding dusk but I must begin.

⁂

Does one not read it in Samuel Beckett's *Murphy*, 'Any fool can turn a blind eye but who knows what the ostrich sees in the sand?' Am I turning into an ostrich, with its brooding and surveying look, destined to see what others can't? Seems like an oddish symmetry. This soliloquy of mine is an exercise in reinventing my imagination, rethinking my cogitations. Every moment this reinvention, rethinking saddles me with its increasing weight. I must rid myself of it; I must pen everything down. What chokes me now will be an uninhibited expression later. I hope so. I must recreate and reconnoitre. An intuitive grasp of the overall significance of human behaviour will be essential in order to come to grips with the sort of understanding that lies behind such behaviour. There are facets that are trivial and those that are intimate; yet all are vital. The paradox of the soliloquy lies there. It allows me a leap from the beginning of the illness to the illness itself. Then, let me lay the bed; facts and fantasies would lie side by side. And yes, any resemblance to reality is a pure coincidence. Let me start my soliloquy with the veering 'I', where you become its witness.

CHAPTER 1

Growing Up in Gorakhpur

Many of us from small places lead an imitated life; a minimalist life. The minimalist existence with vague settings and feelings of inanity helps one to understand paradoxes. Ultimately, everyone stands in awe and listens in darkness, contemplating this existence like I have been doing for the last fifty-seven years. The pacifying effect of contemplation for such a long time lifts me from the floor, takes me towards the sky but never melts me. Sometimes we return to the childhood to get newness. None knows where the beautiful strains of one's music come from. The facts accumulate but I never fall in love with such facts. Indeed, very strangely, I plan to pen the unloved facts.

The place I was esteemed to have been born in was a nameless small town lacking in any worthwhile activity. The early remembrances I had of it was that though small (it is prudent to clarify that I was destined to see bigger places than my birthplace only after I crossed twenty-three-and-a-half years of my life), it was well spread out, thinly populated, very dusty, not very noisy, and relatively dirty with extremes of summer and winter.

I am reminded of a weeping child. No one listens and he slowly drifts into a sobbing mode. Humanity's meekness is in full display. He stops weeping, sobbing. It has been the beauty of my childhood. When I wept, with me wept things I could see—the walls, the earth, utensils, portraits on the wall, broken and not-so-often-used toys, my fingers, my tongue, my toes—everything. But, nothing beyond that. Were my tears, my cries useless?

I, as I was told when I was five years old, had troubled Amma (my mother)—already a mother of seven, three sons and four daughters. All the nine children born to her (the discrepancy between nine and seven is because two died after birth), did cause no extra discomfiture to her and the usual help from the elderly women of the house and support from the locals ensured their arrival within the confines of the house itself. But this time, the pious period of nine months had already passed and it had been over a week post that and still she had not experienced what the doctors refer to as 'labour pain'. At the time, taking expectant mothers to hospitals was considered useless as it was anyway a painful experience. Only after the elderly women in the household jointly ruled out 'delivery inside the house' and forecast imminent danger to the life of mother and child, did the men in charge of such affairs start making arrangements to take the woman to the hospital. The search started for locating a carriage in anticipation, one tonga-wallah was already sounded to be in readiness to be available at a very short notice. But as ill-luck would have it, as soon as the tonga-wallah tried to push the horse, it refused to move as if it had revolted against its use at that unearthly hour. Hectic efforts to make the horse move ended in vain. My uncle who was responsible for bringing the tonga, hurled the nastiest of abuses at the horse, but as wise men don't react foolishly to deeds of the unwise, the horse showed neither any reaction nor any evidence of remorse and remained stubborn. Meanwhile, Amma though not expressing any signs of restlessness, was taken in a rickshaw, fortunately and unexpectedly passing by at that moment, to the government hospital that was three kilometres away from the house. The birth of a child is perceived to be an event full of uncertainties; anything can happen anytime. So was literally true in my case and upon reaching the verandah of the hospital, Amma felt acute pain and after due process, I was born, a full eleven days after the normal period. I, the eighth one.

Dadi (my grandmother), a paralytic, bedridden for more than a decade, unable to move from it unless assisted by two men at least, a task every man in the family shunned, on hearing that I, a son, was born in the family, was reported to have made efforts a few times to move and leave the bed. She failed. Fifty-seven years down the road, I had given this incident ample thought—why had that paralytic woman, eighty years old, endeavoured to raise herself from the bed, unsuccessfully? What did she want to achieve? Was it because a boy had been born in the family?

My birth was accompanied with a grave error. Those who have spent their most valuable time in making observations of how human beings tend to behave have, after detailed scrutiny, proclaimed: To err is human. But, there are errors that are irreversible, necessitating repentance. Sins of the fathers visit upon their children. True, but what about the sins of the nurses, their careless approach to my birth being an example in hand? Who would bear the consequences? Let the error unfold itself. In Hindu religious texts, different codes of conduct are laid down covering almost every activity of a Hindu's life right from his birth to death; there are even prescribed penalties to be suffered in the next life for misconduct committed in the present one.

The local astrologer had conceived of a particular ritual called 'Jatkarm' to be performed before the umbilical cord was severed after delivery of the placenta by the mothers and turmeric applied. This unique ritual was performed during the birth of all my parents' offsprings. But this time, as fortune would ordain it, the delivery was so hasty that the nurse who was assigned the case cut the cord without informing the elderly woman from our family, who were available at the hospital. A very loud and, as the listeners who heard it would describe it later, an extremely strange wail was my first gift to the newly acquired family. And immediately following that wail, I fell into a deep slumber, much to the happiness of the nurse who, after putting me besides my mother, took her leave. Half an hour later came the other elderly members of my family accompanied by an ayah. There was an exhibition of excessive curiosity soon quelled at the nurse's assurance of the successful arrival of the child.

This was the moment where the error was discovered too. The avid ayah whose task it was to cut umbilical cords began to enquire about the person who had substituted her. The inquiry emanated not from any sagacity (and sagacity was a rarity on such occasions) but from her serious concerns about someone eating into her fortunes depriving her of the seventy-five paisa—not a miserly sum in those days—which the parents had to partake as soon as the task was accomplished. Suspecting that the honour had surreptitiously been stolen by the nurse in-charge, the ayah demanded full compensation as no fault could be attributed to her for what had happened. She also blamed the elderly women of our household for unnecessarily hurrying my 'would-be mother' to the hospital. Suspicions travel faster than anything else, leading to many other similar or more complicated suspicions, ensuring a vicious circle that keeps widening and engulfing many an innocent soul in its wake. Only a miracle can possibly save one from that. While the suspected nurse, having obtained the information about the motives being attributed to her, was pondering the finer details she would be required to capsule out in favour of her justified innocence, and not many ideas concrete enough to convince the ayah were forthcoming, she decided to share her thoughts with no one.

One dies to welcome the arrival of another. I was born after two of my sisters had died soon after their birth. My birth washed away the sadness of their deaths completely; there were celebrations. A horde of fifty Brahmins ate three meals that day—three days after my birth—blessing me with blissful life. But, one was more forthcoming. He read my face and palm and benignly pontificated, 'The boy would make a well-read man and may write a few books but will have dirty sexual habits.' That man of accumulated wisdom continued averring, 'People nurture nasty sexual tendencies and many die of syphilis.' He completed the sentence and spat purposefully. My mother was the first to form initial views of the possibility of my wayward personality and the possible disease I would die of. I was three days old. And Amma was reported to have stared at my embryonic genitalia many times during those three days. With much trepidation, I suspect.

The miraculous word 'sex' became a part of my birth and as I voyaged forward into my life. I have had no sex with any woman other than the one I married. But the astrologer's face is the one that lives with me. The squalidity of sex lies in habits.

For my parents, my birth was neither a source of joy nor sorrow; it was the usual nonchalance of parents who suffer everything but lack of children. Mine already had seven. I was another piece of jewel for them—a blank slate, an unfilled brass glass, an object of an empty stare. They never abandoned me but did not own me either; my first experience of truth of life initiating me into my experiments with truths, half-truths and untruths—that enlarged compass within which I keep meandering. Now, I am fifty-seven years old—worthy of the ink a writer uses. The writer loves ink and loves to dip into it. In one such dip, I realized in my birth, I was the only happening. The most unnoticeable cog in the crawling crowd that inhabits the world.

My house was nothing more than an epitome of purposeless

accumulations. Babuji (my father), Amma, brothers, sisters, relatives—all lived independent of each other though logically ours fell in the category of what nuclear families of today fondly recall as joint family. That, for us, meant nothing more than sharing a common sandas (toilet) and kitchen. Leave these two apart and you had people leading scattered lives with no feelings, no emotions, no real relationships. Moreover, every six months or so, a new soul would make its way into the family. I was slowly but steadfastly becoming a part of the larger society which for me was going to define relationships in terms of limitations. Life has been like that all along—restricted by relationships that have been limited to needs.

My Amma feared boarding a train; she feared it would fall off the bridge above the Ganges and everything would be 'destroyed' as she used the word. Towards the last phase of her life, she stopped stepping out of the house. She feared that she might die outside the house she had been residing in for the last sixty years, from where she had moved out for hardly five to ten times in all those years. She had fallen in love with the house among all things. 'Everything would be destroyed—this house, all of you, would be destroyed'—was her usual refrain repeated several times across the day, and even during nights. It would certainly be uttered on waking up in the morning. She used to get up at three in the morning, engulfed in thoughts of despondency and destruction. Her annihilation lay with her; her going out on the train, her fears of the train falling into the river, the bridge collapsing. Falling… collapsing. Things that open outside, beyond the doors of the house—the moving train, the bridge, the house—all shared their agony with her. She survived her fears through her fears.

Babuji hardly displayed any signs of love and affection towards Amma the whole day. However, before he slept, he exhibited supreme urgency and would restlessly call her repeatedly, his voice acquiring greater strength and anger over the course of the calling out. Sometimes my mother came after the needful was done but more often stayed in that room till she was woken up. Foreplay was a luxury; hence forbidden. Haste guided sex; it began that and it ended that. More important things could wait outside and for later—washing utensils, serving food to others in the family and then eating food herself. First father was to be taken care of; he needed a good sleep and for that he needed her. He was the bread earner and she a subject to that, out of a sense of obligation. Consent was taken for granted. Father was rude and crude to his own sons. He would say, 'All you bastards will go to sasural', which was his favourite cry very often coming in the mornings (after he got up), the evenings (after he came back from office) and holidays (throughout those periods). By sasural he meant jail, not one's in-laws.

When it came to social condescension, my father was an equal match to my mother. One early morning, Amma cautioned, 'Áltafwa ke gharwa mat jaiya; woh sab barka ke gosht khate hain.' (Don't go to Altaf's family; they all eat beef.)

Incidentally, I prefer to recall from books that shaped my belief in Hinduism and the Hindu way of life. It is this passage from a chapter titled 'Renaissance or Continuity' from V.S. Naipaul's *India: A Wounded Civilization*. Naipaul, the writer whose love for India endeared him to this country of which he said in the chapter titled 'Synthesis and Mimicry' from the same book that 'India is old, and India continues', writes:

> 'Jamnalal Bajaj, a pious Hindu, was one of Gandhi's earliest financial backers in India. Bajaj died in 1942 and Mrs Bajaj in honour of his memory gave a lot of money to cow-protection societies. Ved Mehta interviewed the old lady for his book *Mahatma Gandhi and His Apostles*. After Gandhi's death, Mrs Bajaj said, she had transferred her loyalty to Vinoba Bhave.

She walked with him for years. Obviously, for the old lady it was very hard, changing camp every day. 'Because,' and here it is her confession, 'I never eat anything I have not prepared with my own hands. Everyone knows that Moslems and Harijans have dirty habits'.

Naipaul concludes: 'And the old lady, who had been chewing something, spat.'

Herein lies the importance of growing up. Amidst books by eminent authors and under illiterate Amma's guidance, insight and foresight, this is what made me.

As Amma rarely ventured out, she never visited any temples while two temples—one of Goddess Kali and the other of Lord Shiva—were situated within the vicinity about a kilometre from my house. There was a small place in my house where a few pebbles were kept as a mark of respect to Lord Shiva. It drew respect from all except my uncle. My mother would pour very clean water as soon as the sun shone in the sky from above her head and invariably put a small petal on it, boarded on which used to be a small quantity of jaggery and camphor.

Were they pebbles? No, they were stones, that Amma worshipped, for many hours, bathing them, pouring oil on them, serving food to them, putting her bowed head on them for several minutes and when angry, banging her head against anything hard cursing her life and folding her hands before the gods to end her life instantaneously. When she banged her head, none was perturbed but my father. He would occasionally remind her to end her 'drama' but this would cause her to bang her head even more violently.

Rains were frequent and heavy in my town. Garbage splayed out in the open at various places and the municipal services hardly cared. Those were the times when corruption was at its height and the staff unions were ineffective. Nearly fifty metres from my house was an intersection joining the narrow lane to the main road. In the corner of that intersection was a place permanently allotted to being used as a garbage dumping site. Some of the residents living in that lane—they were eight to ten—did not have toilet facilities in their houses and while their absence did not deter the grown-ups and adults who utilized the pond and surrounding trees and bushes, dense enough to hide them when easing themselves during early mornings, late evenings and at times even during broad daylight, the real problem came from small children. As is their wont, they felt free to answer the call of nature anytime during the day or night.

Like any other child, I was attracted to objects that appeared strange. One morning, on our way back after buying milk, an object arrested my attention. It was a white piece of thickly wrapped cloth, soaked in blood and since it was not something I had seen before, I could not help directing my queries to my mother who appeared to be least interested in it. I persisted. She looked at it and I could feel she had become angry. 'How on earth do you notice all these ugly things which even men would not like to see? Never make inquiries from anyone about it!' She snubbed me as she twisted my right ear softly. Then, she suddenly asked me to rush and hand over the milk in the house, a task that took me less than a minute, and I returned to find my mother speaking in a hushed tone with two women, both between thirty-five and forty, and both residents of a house adjacent to ours. I could gauge that what transpired between the three women had something to do with the object that had come to my notice earlier. My suspicion was confirmed as at least one of the two women looked backwards to locate the object which, needless to mention, had intensified the desire in me to know about it. It appeared there was some sort of consensus among the three women since while separating, they nodded to each other in agreement about something. The anger on my mother's face had dissipated and in place of it was a kind of satisfaction usually associated with being able to provide convincing arguments. I did not, however, fail to notice the queer look she had as she watched me as if to make out if I was rid of the tremulous obsession over the object. I was not.

Curiosity always thrived in me due to the absence of clear answers. And this is where my uncle proved to be my sounding board. Yes, my go-to person, whom I cherished and looked up to, was my uncle. Like me, he too lived in a world of contrasts. He loved tea. In the absence of wood or coal, my Amma, who had never read anything, burnt pages and pages of complete plays of Shakespeare to prepare tea and my uncle felt a different taste in the tea. He asked for one cup more and it was the turn of yet another scholarly book from my uncle's cupboard.

Early schooling was an extension of the milieu obtaining in my house and neighbourhood. The school consisted of two small rooms: one for the principal and one more teacher and the other for students numbering sixty to seventy all from the same mohalla. The name of the school on a wooden frame hanging loose on the wall behind the principal's chair read Prathamik Pathshala, Dharamshala Bazar, Gorakhpur (Primary School, Dharamshala Bazar, Gorakhpur). It was a school run by the municipality, but it was hardly getting any attention from those responsible for running it, and the task of cleaning the floor and principal's table and chair belonged to one old ayah who was very infrequent with her job. In her absence, the second teacher and in his absence, the principal himself, was seen cleaning the premises. There was big fagged cotton durry covering more than two-thirds of the students' room with five-six holes making the hard uncemented floor very visible. All the students sat there almost touching each other. A huge peepal tree, the age of which was suspected to be more than sixty years, stood tall near the gate of the school and many times, the principal, whenever he willed, gathered all the students there below the peepal tree for PT classes asking one of the students (the monitor) to direct and lead everyone else. Whatever physical gestures he performed, we repeated without being aware of what we were doing. One thing the students knew, that but for these physical movements, they wouldn't pass the exams.

The principal, whose name I forget, was a slightly obese dhoti-kurta wearing gentleman and fond of teaching in a particular way—he would cry at the peak of his voice when teaching us the Hindi alphabet, '*Bolo bachchon, Ka ke baad Kha, Kha ke baad Ga, Ga ke baad Gha...*' (Say, children, Kha after ka; Ga after kha; Gha after Ga...). For numbers, again his voice would be at its peak, '*Do duni char; char duni aath; aath duni solah...*' (2×2=4; 4×2=8; 8×2=16...) That was his way of introducing his students to the world of words and numbers. He expected a louder repetitive response from students and on that not forthcoming, would sharply snub, '*Kya tum sab bhuke pet ayen hoi? Kal se khakar aana nahi to mat aana.*' (Have all of you come without taking food? From tomorrow, come with your belly full or don't come.) There was a blackboard on the wall but he hardly used it and relied on his vocal strength which he was amply gifted with. Contrary to the principal, the other teacher was more interested in serving the principal: fetching the latter's lunch box and afternoon tea from his house. Many times in the evenings, I saw him bringing vegetables, etc., from the market and transporting these to the principal's house. In modern parlance, I wouldn't hesitate calling him as the principal's factotum. In the principal's absence—that was really rare—the second one would substitute with his thin voice. He was an unenthusiastic fellow. It was a big relief for us students. The range of the principal's expressions was far more varied and direct than that of the second one.

Within a fortnight of my entry in that school, I was identified to be a very poor student. I was admitted there six months after classes started and thus was lagging behind by six months compared to other students. A week after I joined the school, the students had to take their first test and obviously I was a loser. Question papers were served along with two sheets on which I, like others, was supposed to write. Very embarrassed to find almost all writing something on their answer scripts under the watchful eyes of the principal, I also attempted answers even without realizing what I was doing. But, the principal looked pleased and when my uncle visited the school to collect me in the evening, he also felt happy finding the principal patting my back in recognition of my having attempted the questions despite having joined recently. In the house a general happiness pervaded for a few hours in celebration of the excellence I had shown in the examination. However, many members seemed unconvinced.

Three days later, results were declared and much to my family's chagrin, I got a zero. Disappointing as it was, it was not acceptable at least to my uncle who had used his influence to get the principal to show him my answer scripts. I had copied all the questions from the question paper onto the answer script. Upon reaching home, a resounding slap on my face was accompanied with my uncle telling my mother, '*Din ka sapna dekhna band karo aur isko ghar baithao. Iske kismet me juta polish karna likha hai.*' (Stop daydreaming and let him sit in the house. It is in his destiny to polish the shoes.) My first encounter with examinations resulted in a resounding slap with not such a sweet pontification.

Nights and days make for unenviable company. I go back again in time. I reflect back, it was my classroom and there was a chair in it, beyond repair. It was like the lot of us, about sixty—we were beyond repair. Like that chair, the ayah, aged seventy, the principal, the teacher—both jaded, poor, wearing undistinguished clothes, thin and weak, fragile and weird—and then the uncontrollable crowd of noisy, ill-mannered, directionless, suffocating, sixty children never interested in what was to come next. All 'beyond repair'. An illusory world of disbelief pervaded us; a sense of nihilism gripped us. I noticed for the first time only circles and circles—from the tiniest to the largest, from the thinnest to the waxiest, from one to many, from many to one—circles only.

Now, it is time that my soliloquy must move on to Professor Yadav and my uncle—two big influences in my life.

CHAPTER 2

Early Adolescence: Professor Yadav and My Uncle

Allen Ginsberg wrote: 'The sadness is, that every leaf has fallen before.'

Gorakhpur then, was an epitome of Ginsbergian pessimism.

These words make me realize that societies struggling to come to proper shape thrive on assumptions governing them and when it comes to describing my birth place, I will go with the assumptions, even naïve ones, of the place, for realities divorced from such assumptions, when reflected upon, irrespective of when that happens, portray distortions in experienced realities.

∽

I spent the first twenty-three years of my life—the most important formative years in any individual's life—in my home town, Gorakhpur. On my later visits, what welcomed me there amidst many things—usual and unusual—were memories that had been quiescent but kept coming back to me sporadically, given the number of times I would encounter them: the streets, the shops, the colleges, the schools, the University, the vendors, the hospitals, the libraries and above all the individuals that crowded the city.

These encounters brought a somewhat cumulatively animated revival and reminder of the past which I wish to record now.

During my Master's, many of my teachers, including some who taught me economics, behaved like bewildered and haphazard creatures although they assumed much authority and glory given their thorough grounding in academia. That was a belief they lulled themselves into. This perception, as I discovered, was erroneous. In fact, there was no difference between a teacher about to retire and one who had just started teaching. They shared the same perceptions, the same value systems and above all the same psychic make-up. Their vision was a shared vision, the one unsusceptible to any change. Nothing was imagined deeply and textbooks were half-dead in their hands. They believed in actions aimed at destroying the meagre creativity in any student. An intelligent student was successfully dragged into an abundance of puny-headedness. They believed in absolute falsity of the questions, the answers to which lay beyond the hackneyed boundaries of textbooks. They were serious enough not to keep a record of anything. They loved acts of ignominy that suited their temperament well. Though they served academic institutions, their belief lay in the uselessness of time: everything including knowledge and learning would vanish one day. It was instant life they reposed their faith in; things to happen later had no value for them.

1979. One day, I enquired from Dr Shukla about the concept economists call 'money illusion'. I had read of it in Don Patinkin's book *Money, Interest and Prices*. 'What is money illusion, sir?' I asked politely. His answer left me baffled. '*Packetwa mein kuch baki wasey hi thonk dela*. "Money illusion" *unke liya hai jiske pocketwa mein kuchh ola aur tohre jaise daridra ke liya nahin*.' (Do you have some money in your pocket or just ask questions like that?

'Money illusion' is for those who have money in their pocket and not for paupers like you.) Dr Gupta was more humble. He admitted at least half-truths. *'Jyada prasanwa mat pucha. Gharwa mein mehrarua tang kareli, yehan to kum se kum, chain sey ziye da.'* (Don't ask many questions. My wife makes life hell for me in the house. At least let me live peacefully here.)

I have learnt everything in life but not in a conventional way.

1979–80. In the intensely caste-ridden atmosphere at the Gorakhpur University, my solace, surprisingly, came from the young (I guess he was then thirty-five or so) and thoughtful Professor Yadav with his drooping beard covering what students believed to be his scarred visage. His gait gave an impression that his extended upper portion was propelling him forward while the lower part of his body was glued to the ground. So, we perceived him as moving while he stood still and vice versa. At the university he was perhaps the only Yadav professor. And chuckles from not only the students but also the creamy-layered professors were a common sight. Have I myself not faced such scoffs so many times thus far? Professor Yadav's sense of disenchantment and detachment from those creamy-layered professors lacking both wisdom and knowledge endeared him to me so much that I made him my mentor. On notions not clear to me, I would be one with him with his further enlightening notions. He was brilliance unto himself. His company has been very favourable to me in terms of sharing thoughts and juxtaposing countervailing versions and his wise commentaries on issues from metaphysics to masturbation.

A visit to the past makes one judge how far societies have moved, and how matured, well-behaved they have become. It was in 1980 that I did my Master's in Economics from Gorakhpur University and like many other students, I was also seized with the apprehension about the prospects in the days to come. To overcome that, I went to meet late Dr B.K. Singh, head of the department of economics, entreating him to accept me as his research scholar in their PhD programme. His stern looks matched his equally firm and icy voice, 'What will you do after that? Go back and prepare for competitive examinations.' The end was nearly complete. The time to stay with languid feelings of being an unemployed youth, in a lower middle-class family, losing precious moments of life had come. However, unfortunately, after that I could never meet late Dr Singh.

Times were different. Strange considerations caused one to make bizarre decisions. So was the case with the opening of a degree college about which this was in the air: the degree college was opened by a rich man in order to offer a job to a young man who was reportedly going to be his prospective son-in-law. Unaware of this immutable relationship in the offing, I applied for the post of a lecturer in that college. A few of my 'well-wishers' approached me with sagacious advice asking me not to appear for the interview as there was only one post. I declined. The day of reckoning was unlike other days and the interview board was headed by none other than the same Dr B.K. Singh. Although determined to offer the job based on merit, he felt tied by the obligation towards keeping to the owner's promise to the prospective son-in-law. He refused to succumb to pressure and declined to conduct the interview. Later, a new board was formed; this time headed by another gentleman, flexible enough, from some other university. The gentleman heading the board asked me about the difference between economic growth and economic development. Realizing that the die had already been cast, I decided to give my best and tried to explain the difference by citing the concept of 'instrumental value premises' enunciated by economist Gunnar Myrdal further amplifying it by citing ten indices of economic development again as suggested by Myrdal and their relevance to Adelman and Morris's forty-eight qualitative indicators applicable to developing countries. I could sense the disquieted demon of 'holier than thou' syndrome raising its head in the room as the learned members seemed to be the least interested in what I was mouthing. Obviously they might have been a bit miffed. Then, another member asked what the aim of economic development in the context of Gorakhpur, the city, should be. Another economist of eminence, Paul Streeten, came to my rescue. 'Transformation of human beings is the ultimate objective of economic development. Gorakhpur requires transformation of human beings.' By that time, the level of discomfort was at its summit and the chairman of the board told me very curtly that the interview was over and I must leave. I left with Dr B.K. Singh's icy words ringing in my ears, 'What will you do after that? Go back and prepare for competitive examinations.' I realized the pivotal message given to me by the Professor—he placed his belief in competitions as a relatively fairer means to have one's talent scrutinized. So did I.

In 2017, I visited my birthplace again. It was my last visit to the place and what impacted me the most was the relevance of the question learned members of the interview board asked me and the reply I had given in the interview several years back. Society grows only when human beings realize the need for transformation, yearn, by all means feasible, to achieve that transformation and be prudent enough to see logic in the steps taken towards such transformation and to accept them. A society which lacks the power to question itself, to confront itself with the questions so bare as not to escape even the blindest of eyes and to seek answers to such questions, and which feels incapacitated enough to assess itself is a society where such a transformation which economists like Paul Streeten cogitate is met with maximum resistance. Individuals need no safety-valve; they are comfortably ensconced in their daily routine shunning any disturbance. They want their world reflected in others' but never others' in their own. The idea of not looking beyond oneself is the most lucrative idea as it bars the possibility of interpretation—the possibility of having a renewed look at one's interpretations of oneself or the way one looks at things around.

In my conversation with a senior journalist of a national Hindi newspaper who had spent a few years in Gorakhpur during roughly the same time as I had, my ideas got pepped up—the place had been, not to speak of stagnating, actually going downhill. We tried to remember Gorakhpur as it existed almost thirty-five years back and we were approaching the discussion from the students' points of view as at least some of them might prove to be marvels of the city in the future. He fondly recollected about the bookstall, a medium-sized shop in the heart of the town, the only shop selling important magazines like *The Sunday, Illustrated Weekly of India, Caravan* and many others and further recollected how the big moustached owner of the stall, had an equally big heart and was always forthcoming to help curious students by arranging books and magazines for them. What was abstruse, started clearing up; I too was a regular visitor of that bookstall and the jovial face of the owner reappeared before me. 'Where is he?' I asked. 'You should visit the bookstall in the evening,' the journalist's dimmed voice spoke. I had to board the flight to Delhi the following day. 'So I ought to meet him this evening itself,' I thought.

The bookstall used to be located in front of one of the two cinema theatres located side by side in Golgher, then considered to be the poshest area of Gorakhpur. Books and magazines in the stall used to illumine the mind of every student capable of fathoming the value of books. It was seven in the evening. Traffic in front of the theatres was very dense—almost impenetrable. I reached up to where the stall used to be; everything seemed hazed. The bookstall was nowhere in sight; there were large concrete structures instead. I really felt guilty.

Later, I came to know that the bookstall had very much been

there but it had been reduced to a most inconspicuous existence—an example of concrete structures replacing places of knowledge and learning. Development entails costs. And what about my big moustached and even bigger hearted bookstall-owner?

Once in 2005, I remember visiting Gorakhpur. This was before my last visit to the place in 2017. Professor Yadav was talking about the status of libraries in colleges, there had been hardly any funds for books. The books there were, had been bought years back but not issued to any student or teacher. Very few students used to enter the library since, barring the library, there were attractions galore inside the campus. The nonchalant nature of teachers was further insult to injury. Everyone was content with 'kunji' or 'key-books' with limited or almost no desire for main textbooks. Everything was in complete disarray. 'But why did not the person in charge of the library or the librarian ask for funds or raise the other issues you just spoke about?' I asked him. 'He wouldn't do that. His seniors and colleagues would warn him of possible consequences. He might be asked to explain his utility to the college: how he is useful to the college when books bought are not in demand. You are a bureaucrat. I suppose you know how systems work, how mirrors are diverted.' I found the Professor very straightforward and facile. He was successful in making a point. He continued further, 'People have no trouble with the form; they know the art of fitting into particular forms as these suit them. But, they have complaints about the way systems work. Why to blame the librarian? Or even the system?' the Professor effortlessly concluded.

There are no empty spaces in the city. Places meant for public rendezvous, where children used to play and old people used to spend mornings and evenings sharing time together, are completely and mechanically filled. There is a definite pattern—doctors' clinics, adjacent to which are privately-run hospitals, adjacent to which are medical stores and then coaching centres for MBBS and JEE. The view of the number of patients waiting in queues outside is simply choking. Their patience harrowing; many times their turn might not come the same day. The vicious circle continues. Students getting trained to pass MBBS examinations are opening more clinics, hospitals, medical shops—the chain, a robust one, is already in place.

In the mohalla called Sumer Sagar, where I spent my childhood and early adulthood and where walking, running or even playing on narrow roads were easy and comfortable, I found narrow roads that had become narrower; not even two square feet space was available on either side of those roads. Everything was perfectly occupied, congested with people. Fabulous cars families dream of: rickshaws, auto-rickshaws, scooters, motorcycles, bicycles, umpteen number of pedestrians—all vying with each other to make a movement forward. Every movement seemed calculated; there was no sense of relief. Their patience was really distressing. It took me forty minutes by car to cover a distance of thousand metres. 'Har sham yeh numayis dekh sakten hain yahaan,' (Every evening this exhibition can be seen here) my co-passenger said and then laughed boisterously. None seemed to take note of either what he said or his boisterous laughter. But I was onto something else.

∫

It was 1978. There were, as it seems to me even now, not much political activity in the area I grew up in, though unions in colleges and university had in them more mischief-mongers than persons of calibre and talent. The only remembrance I have of such activity in my area is when the municipal representative from the concerned ward came out addressing a tiny crowd of less than fifty fellows, hurling choicest abuses on the district collector for not removing a carcass of a dog rotting in front of his house. They were guided less by the genuine requirements of the students and more by their casteist inclinations. They had the blessings of mafia lords who gave Gorakhpur a distinct identity. The mafia lord had reportedly once murdered his counterpart in broad daylight when the latter was getting down from his bike to honour an invitation from the former. The city got a name, a name one would be ashamed of. I heard a conversation between two well-read teachers of my college:

'Second Chicago.'
'Second Chicago.'
'Show me on the map.'
'Look there.'
'Second Chicago.'
'Out there.'
'In India.'
'In that corner.'
'You mean bordering Nepal.'
'Yes, be proud of it. We are from there.'
'Where?'
'Second Chicago.'
'You call it Gorakhpur.'
'Who named that place that?'
'That place named itself that.'
'You mean Gorakhpur named itself Second Chicago?'

These were the great inhabitants of that tiny place! Afflicted by poverty, violence, sex trade, caste prejudices and suppressed people—this was Gorakhpur, my home town.

The three decades I spent in Gorakhpur since 1960 were scary years. Now, the hardcore mafias have mellowed or rather transformed. The dreaded mafia lords have grown old, and a few of them have turned themselves into acclaimed thinkers, social analysts and social reformers, each reportedly lording over an empire of more than Rs 500 crore. Above everything else, they form the secular pillars of Gorakhpur. Both Hindus and Muslims go to them together to seek their blessings. The young girls they used to bed in their heyday are there living in silence, while the dreaded mafia lords have become harmless cogs. They can do nothing but wait for their end. That's the power of time, of age and of retribution.

Enamoured with new models, modern developmental economists now fascinatingly talk of 'human thriving' and 'functionings' as indices of development. Economist G.A. Cohen explains these concepts by saying that the life a person leads can be seen as a combination of 'doings' and 'beings' which can be generically called 'functionings'. These 'functionings' accrue from elementary matters such as being well-nourished and free from disease and also accrue from complex matters such as having self-respect, human dignity, participating in community life, etc. In brief, these modern concepts, heavily influenced by John Rawls' and Ronald Dworkin's philosophical outpourings, connote how people conduct their lives, how and what quality of health and medical services they enjoy, the nature and quality of education available to them, how labour is rated—whether it is rewarding or monotonous, how citizens conduct their social and personal relations, how familial and sexual relations are structured, how societies permit their inhabitants to imagine, to have feelings like love, appreciation and gratitude. All these modern indices of development were what perhaps Paul Streeten had in view though not in as articulated a form as available in economic literature today, when he equated economic development with 'transformation of human beings'.

When one looks back at the past, one looks at it with a hope that things must have travelled forward and a bigger clearer world will be in sight. As I initiated myself into services, a senior bureaucrat with a mischievous smile, buttonholed me, 'So you are from Gorakhpur—the place known for mafia gangs and encephalitis?'

'Yes, of course sir, but also for the Gita Press, the famous Gorakhnath temple, literary legends like Munshi Premchand, Firaq Gorakhpuri, learned men like Dr Raghuvir Singh known in the sphere of political science, and many more,' I responded.

'Yeah, I see but that is not the point,' his meek voice accompanied a smile, the nature of which, I must admit, I have not been able to unravel thus far; it was like 'what' or 'that is not the point'. But his question introduced me to another question: the question of visiting and revisiting the concept of self-definition. Should one stand where one stood decades back? Should one not seek a more exquisite self-definition? Should one not strive for a bigger world—an altered world?

Economic development does not lie in figures set forth in tabular forms alone nor is it achieved in terms of haphazard growth of roads, schools and colleges, clinics, hospitals, medical shops, coaching centres, schools and old-age homes. All these are required but in a planned manner. Commercial relations don't explain and end economic development. Statistical tables cannot narrate all stories. They sometimes contain facades—commercial and conceptual ones. To me, Gorakhpur seems like a box-diagram of international economic theory: one box with one equal size box superimposed over it. People, crowds, events, happenings, stories all tightly packed inside. The group dynamics at its nadir, its vision considerably obscured. Movement should be in terms of creation of physical assets which no doubt is a herculean task with long 'fruition-effects' given meagre developmental efforts during the last decades. What is really more herculean is how not to allow concrete structures define and determine the nature and the character of the city; how to make students visit libraries very often and at least have a look at the books; how to make ordinary citizens, the most marginal of men, enjoy 'human functionings' making them capable of feeling life, to love it, to draw pleasure out of it. The senior journalist, the professor, the librarian, the co-passenger in the car whose wont was to laugh uproariously for no reason or rhyme, the bureaucrat who had evolved himself to judge people in terms of the uglier facets of the place they were born and raised in, the members of the interview board getting perplexed at the mere mention of names like Myrdal, Streeten, Adelman and Morris, and many, many more from the general populace like them can hardly be said to have enjoyed much of 'human thrivings' or 'functionings'.

Henry David Thoreau is known for his experiments in the art of simple living, bringing nature very close to it in order to 'front only the essential facts of life'. Gorakhpur needs answers derived off of collected perceptions. The common people need a leader to guide them through those perceptions to reach a path. Gorakhpur needs a Siddhartha, it needs peace. It needs a day which, a la Thoreau, is 'an epitome of a year'. We are waiting for the time Gorakhpur will swallow the worst facets of its past and drawing from its vast spiritual, religious, historical and literary past, factor in elements from its marvellously gargantuan heritage into a holistic developmental model for the city and make headway towards a new dawn. Let us wait for that new dawn for only that dawn will be able to cope with the pessimistic Ginsbergian outlook.

∽

Some time back, one night while dining, I thought of the thin, weary, bearded, dirty old man sitting in a corner on an otherwise empty road; he seemed to be staring into a void, which, by all means, was absent, but the old man had chosen that corner to detect the void and fixated his gaze on it. To me, he seemed to be the most secure man in the world with no interest in any movements or activities. For wasn't his security not a prime motivator for him? The mere fact of his staying nowhere or somewhere, he knew not where, or the fact that no one else was sure of the world to which he belonged did not deter him from fixing his gaze onto an arena in which his entire world existed. He felt so secure of himself, of his precepts and his belongings, he would possibly not lose the edge of his survival. So sated was he. He abhorred any transformation; reposing his trust in his retreat and inching forward was a completely blocked choice. I was sure he must have bathed months ago, not trimmed his beard for months, and no food or drinks must have attracted him. Did he not perhaps require some psychiatric help? Amidst such remembrances a fleeting thought came to me—that of a bureaucrat-turned-poet and his conversation on national TV, 'My poems are about psychoanalysis. Okay. See this poem: this is definitely psychoanalysis.' I was amazed at the interviewer's sense of belief (or relief) when the poet stressed the word 'psychoanalysis'. Then ensued his sagacious reading of what he fondly referred to as 'excerpts from one of my favourite poems'. Extremely narrow and unauthentic ones lacking aesthetic vigilance. It was all a sham. He seemed to have developed, unknowingly, a taste for knowledge but lacked completely the vision and wisdom essential for such knowledge to come to fruition. He was a poet who knew neither his words nor his ideas but only 'psychoanalysis'. Such poets have great potential to become a problem unto themselves; they revolve around this problem and then succumbing to it, let the problem guide them throughout their literary career.

But let us get back to the old man!

This image of the strange-looking old man with no urge and zeal to show any movement and respond to any upheavals is still with me. My goodness, what have I said! Do I know the excruciating pain and upheavals inside his otherwise calm demeanour? Sometimes, I look at myself. Even a small jerk around me sends a tremor down my spine. I am pained when I am criticized unwontedly; I feel like rebelling when confronted with a farrago of untruths that bewitches critics. Don't you think we are forced into a quagmire of relations born out of perceptions founded on plain belief in the exploitation of silence? It springs up from lewdness of minds? On the contrary, this old man took no notice of noises, aberrations and explosions. As I observed, he felt totally free of the relationship he had with his surroundings. A donkey with a saintly composure beside him brayed continuously for some time but to no avail. The man kept relishing his aloneness and the gaze into nullity.

One day, Professor Yadav and I were at his place and he was clear, 'He was too much into himself. As of now…as of now…then, yes, of course. There what you called. Nothingness. Most phoney word. Nonsensical. Extravagant description. Nothingness is an extravagant description. Words collude to kill all hopes. Bloody fools.' He was scratching his left ear.

With whimsicality in his eyes and unascertainable firmness on his face, Professor Yadav tried to sip tea from the cup but it was too hot for his swollen and darkish lips. The creamy thin layer glued to his lips, he literally struggled for some time to get rid of it. He chewed it once and succeeded in pushing it inside his mouth. Aware of my presence, Professor Yadav kept himself busy enough in books with his hands turning page after page, absent-mindedly, though he himself was sure he intended to locate nothing in particular. Once he bemused his students by telling them he found nothing in pages of books and if he found anything of any significance, then he would lose it as soon as he would close reading the book. 'Everything gets buried as soon as anything worthwhile is closed. Rediscovery is possible only through buried wisdom. That is human mind's greatest virtue. Ignorance is its biggest asset. All great minds were ignorant minds who sought prominence through their temporal existence. Only one activity is not the sole activity of the mind. Mind works best while in vacuum.' He argued and this time Professor Yadav was addressing an audience. That was once upon a time.

But now turning to the old man's problem, Professor Yadav had the following to offer, 'I have read excerpts from your notebook. I think that without pure being or pure consciousness, nothingness cannot be conceived. When one is in a state of pure consciousness, there are no thoughts but when one is fast asleep, there are no thoughts too. Was the old man you saw sleeping or was he conscious then? How did you reach the conclusion? That old man was in a state of thoughtlessness which accrued to him due to his being in a continual flux of intense thoughts.

What was that old man? Was he not the most unnoticeable creature in a crowd we call the world? Undoubtedly a poet can have many consciousnesses and thank goodness for that. I guess I have inanimate objects in my mind when I think of that old man as some sort of consciousness. A glass is a glass unless it is invested with some voice by a poet. And while a cat may not have human consciousness, it has some. There are no doubts. But that old man's behaviour piques my curiosity. Science cannot explain human consciousness the way your observation of that old man does.' Professor Yadav was damn serious. He always was. I felt appeased.

∽

I move now to my uncle, my father's brother. He left the world at sixty-seven also leaving behind his memories in a 4/3 frame in which hangs his black and white photograph taken ten years before he passed away. He led a life devoid of glee. My uncle applied to himself the principle of exclusion—denial; he denied him to himself. For him, God was the greatest curse on this earth. This I could know as he took me through Mephistopheles and how Dr Faustus rose to fame through him. If you permit me to hazard a guess, he blamed God for his father's violent death; by violent I don't mean death in an accident or by accident but a death that tortures slowly, I mean the death which is certain but annoying. My uncle unfortunately seemed to believe that his happiness lay in living on the strength of his illusions and he lived and died with those illusions. He also died a bachelor.

His room was a dilapidated space exuding cold curiosity. The first thing I come across on opening the lock and entering the room is my uncle; he is no more, I know that. You seem worried, confused, that is unbecoming of you. A dead man cannot be alive, there is no philosophy behind it; it is a fact that through fiction, writers of seminal importance enliven dead beings often. Photographs save memories from gradual death; so, it is my uncle's photograph that I meet every time I enter the room. Ensconced in a 1980 wooden frame, it hangs comfortably on the wall facing the inner door. Things never amused him; he had the same facial expression throughout the year. I could never see any significant variations there. He had no problems with himself; he lived something he never seemed to deny but in his living there was no life—he did not quite exist, he lived but without, he lived unknowingly. There was nothing to move him forward, to compel him unto himself—it was he, sans himself.

Nothing surprised him; he was beyond things that were capable of astonishing anyone. He was heading towards the end of his life in a manner similar to the one with which he had travelled thus far. His path was safe; he preferred safety to anything that he feared might take him for a ride. He lived like a corpse and he loved me as if I was one too; so it was ice-like, the love from a corpse towards his adopted son.

The other day, Professor Yadav, as promised, got to explaining my uncle's traits which, because of my close bond with my uncle, I could not be expected to even gauge, nor to share. Professor Yadav never failed to keep his word.

'I feel KK, your uncle simply existed, but did he really live? That is something I am not sure of. There are issues your uncle seemed to have and these lie at the root of matters concerning your uncle's life. I have often been bewitched and thwarted by this relationship between existence and the willingness, or the absence of it, to live it. This relationship seems to have been the hotbed of varied speculations by philosophers—trapped in the echo-chambers of their own existence, trying to resolve the dazzling dilemma hidden in what I said just now: your uncle existed but did not live. For some people, mere existence is necessary—to live or not to do so comes later. Your uncle was aware of the risks/dangers of his existence—his cherished desire to obtain freedom and independence and further liberating himself from the shackles binding him to his past. Vagaries of nature and time, more often than not, must have landed him to an island of uncertainty and he might have found his defences weak, baffling and bridling. He was a man without options who succumbed mutely to all ailments. In his life, he experienced: illness, temptations, death of loved ones/enemies, the loss of things we don't want to lose.' Professor Yadav's voice was reticent but firm. And his assertions such as to keep me on alert. 'Do you know Roquentin? Have you read Sartre's *Nausea*?' He doubted if my uncle was seized with existential concerns and propositions. 'Sartre's Roquentin faces dilemmas throughout, "But there it is. You can't say that that exists, that spinning record exists, the air struck by the vibrating voice exists... I who am listening, I exist. Everything is full, existence everywhere...there is this...this rigour". Or look at this, "That is living. But when you tell about life, everything changes; only it is a change nobody notices"'. Professor Yadav described my uncle as 'a heap of existents,' who must have felt superfluous in relation to others. My uncle's fears were inbuilt in Roquentin's question, 'I've stopped writing my book...it is finished; I can't go on writing it. What I am going to do my life?'

Then my uncle had problems of choice and freedom which may not be available to all and equally. After all, he was a proclaimed bachelor.

Professor Yadav accused my late uncle of having suffered from the conflict between reason and faith. Then he was silent for more than five minutes, during which time I was drawn towards his facial expressions but his beard offered me a tough battle and I surrendered.

'Bachelors and spinsters are doomed to enjoy neither reason nor faith; they enjoy themselves. And sometimes their counterparts.' Having said this, Professor Yadav excused himself leaving me in a quandary. The impasse had not been very easy for me to deny.

27 April 2014. Today I am thinking of what the learned Professor wanted to connote by his words inspiring inquiry. Do married couples have the most reconciled state of equilibrium with them? Do they suffer no conflict between reason and faith? Or between faith and reason? How will you account for failed marriages? Will poke Professor Yadav about it later. I would like to see him again breathing his own breath, at one with himself.

In retrospect, I feel one of the vaguely felt reasons why uncle was like the way he was, is what I am writing of him now. It must have been his inability to distance himself from the house or family members most of whom he thought of as 'vultures in wait' but never wore his heart on his sleeve. On many occasions he threatened to leave the house and twice or thrice did so too but a few days later, came back. There were scandalous rumours that said he visited and stayed with a Muslim woman with whom he was suspected to have closeness of an unmentionable type. Family members did try to locate how to please him but then that task was well-nigh impossible. The unpleasant atmosphere inside the house, lack of interest in others' welfare, neglect of weak and ill women—two or three, unhygienic habits particularly in the kitchen—all rolled into one to make a sensitive person like uncle sick—of both the milieu and himself. Though I might not be favourably inclined to go along Professor Yadav's unappetizing estimate of uncle who died in 1993, I value Professor's critique, for such critiques provide a robust ground for future assessments of individuals. The value of his photograph leads me to one unique purpose: magnanimity of life ought to be for others—the weaker people rather than one's own self. As for Professor Yadav and myself, readers will be knowing more as they proceed further with the book.

CHAPTER 3

Rendezvous With a New World

Early eighties. In any story involving success or failure, envelopes, that too sealed ones, play a vital role. They are supposed to guide the chaps whose fates are sealed inside to a voyage towards an altered world and mind. A wait for twenty-three-and-a-half years, a wait through the fragility of a marginalized life and a stream of hopelessness, a wait an unyielding life has been subjugating me to—all seem to have gathered that one particular moment in the anticipation of what might be in that unopened envelope which I supposed was going to be harbinger of some change to my fate. The day arrived. The envelope conveyed to me my success in the civil services examination. An exalted opinion of my scholarship was established at least for me. Time to step into another world—a world of ethics and ethos, a world that ought to bolster any stranger, but instead is one that distinguishes wheat from chaff or vice versa. Hands that are soiled are the hands that inherit the task of shaping and initiating, for better or worse. Fate is so crude.

2015. How many years gone? Faced with the burden of memories, I wish I could recall that. It seems as if an enormous amount of time has passed by. For many days, almost two months or more, I have been at a loss to write anything. Not even a word. Many times I have opened my diary thinking I would start but I have not been able to go any further. In retrospect, I feel many ideas were there, hanging in the air; they came near me almost touching the edges of my brain that prod one to write but they left having failed to make further inroads. I complained of this inability to write to one of my writer friends who heard me with fascination, his acute thoughtfulness on display and then came this advice: 'Go to some harlot. Any one will do. Sensitive writers find harlots sexually very satisfying and intellectually very stimulating. If you trust me, try the ones in business for quite some time—eight to eleven years. They are very free, unreserved, you know.'

I carried books with me; they gave me company. I never visited harlots—considered by many as easy availabilities—for company; never call girls and never gays. In fact, I got all of them in the books I read. I talked to them too. I would scribble in the corners of the books—scribbles that even an hour later, I was unable to decode, and so I thought over them some more trying to make out the meaning hidden in the words and sentences I had written. But I could reach nowhere.

A writer looks for clues for the beginning. And what better way than to hear honest confessions of a harlot-seeker: my writer friend.

Many times, I had heard my uncle murmuring a phrase: 'unfortunate fellow'. Seeing none in the vicinity, I guess the term was meant to welcome me; filling the air with pungent fervour. My rendezvous with the new world indicated to me some principles; I really learnt, while moving within the new world. It can happen to anyone, anywhere: at any home, any school, any college, any university, any centre of learning and training. The first principle of collective ethos is to judge people and judge them from the very beginning, to keep at bay those sufficiently gifted with insight to pierce through the veneer or the facade of faces. The herds are assiduous followers. What is wrong if I hold my thoughts high enough beyond the reach of the 'common rut'? But am I alone in this journey? No. There are many spectators languishing in silence. Collective ethos survives on a sense of evenness and unevenness. But can that be let to pass. Implicit questions have got to be answered.

Let me now take you to some halos of power corridors. Power has its own anatomy, its own patterns. Everywhere it is the same. Either in the real or imagined world. The anatomy of power has many inbuilt and implicit questions that have got to be answered.

1987–88. I reported at the Institute of Learning and Wisdom for honing my behavioural skills.

I came face-to-face with a big brass nameplate—

Dr Biswa M. Bhowmic
Vice-Principal (Second-in-Command)
Institute of Learning and Wisdom
Maranda.

I read it as I ushered myself into his chamber.

Many cardinal principles regulate civilized society and one such is: Seniority determines the kind and degree of humiliation you can heap onto your juniors.

'Your name please,' asked the stout man, balding with burning heavy-lidded eyes. He was second-in-command in the institute waiting for his already delayed elevation to being first-in-command. He had a curious reputation of being a biased and prejudiced being, soft with some—particularly girls and women, spinsters and married alike—and harsh with young gentlemen. To say it differently, he had no qualms using his abrasives with some to amuse others. He took extreme pride in his seniority in hierarchy and lost no opportunity in implementing that pride. Already, overawed by the reputation of the gentleman I was to report to, I did not notice any courtesy in him to have a glance at me so far. I meekly submitted, 'Sir, my name is K.K. S...'

'What a bemusing name? Repeat it again,' the second-in-command laughed full-throatily.

I repeated.

'Do you know why shoes have laces?' the question left me gobsmacked as I had never expected this type of a question. I chose not to reply. In fact I had not understood the question. Sorry. This infuriated him and he raised his otherwise already loud voice still further.

Second cardinal principle: I cannot be the one to choose. Servants can't be choosers. Beggars cannot ask questions but they ought to answer, even if they don't know the answers. Silence deserves punishment, lack of knowledge, appreciation and upward mobility.

'Look at your shoe. Left one. See the laces. They are not tied. Don't you have basic courtesy? Courtesy of being properly attired before you depose. Before a senior officer.'

'I am extremely sorry, sir. I never meant to be discourteous. I can never even dream of it.' I allowed the realization to dawn upon me. The shoelace was not properly tied. I cursed the nylon lace. They are so not dependable.

'Sit down. Sit down. Where do you come from?'

'Sir, Gorakhpur.' I saw a smile on second-in-command's face though I found it hard to fathom its nature.

'Gorakhpur. I think I have heard of it. It is the place children die of encephalitis. You know, encephalitis means brain fever… Hope you never got it,' he was sneaky.

'Yes sir. No sir.'

'What a backward place. When did you leave it?'

'A week back. I left it on the night of 17th and reached here on the 20th.'

'No, baba, I mean when did you leave it for your studies? Which college and university did you attend for your graduation and post-graduation?'

'Sir, I graduated from a local college and post-graduated from Gorakhpur University.'

'Really. It's news to me that the place has a university too. What is your caste? I mean, are you from general category?'

'Yes sir, I am a Kayastha.'

'Good, good, and your basic discipline in post-graduation?'

'Economics.'

'So you are an MA in Economics from Gorakhpur University.' This time I saw a smile on his face and found it contemptuous.

'Yes, sir.'

'Tell me the names of some of your professors. I mean, those who taught you.'

'Dr Singh, Dr Pandey, Dr Shukla, Dr Prasad, Dr Ram and Professor Yadav.'

'No Bengali teachers. Still you passed civil services examination? You know, unless one is taught by a Bengali teacher, one hardly knows economics. I, myself—a Bengali and a student of economics—will tell you this.'

'There was one—Mr Ganguly. He taught us History of Economic Thought—a very lacklustre subject. It hardly attracts me. It never attracts anybody.'

'Be brief. Don't talk much. You are too young. And yeah, you have a singer also from that place. A qawwal. I forget the name.'

'Rangeen, sir. Pappu Rangeen. He sings local songs in the local dialect. Have you heard of him? I have his audio cassette.'

'Are you crazy? Do you think such type of nameless singers would be worth my attention?'

'I am sorry, sir, but I know only of him.'

'What nonsense! You don't even know that qawwal from your

place. The gentleman I have in mind is the one who sings in Urdu. You people call such fellows qawwal.'

'Oh, got it. You are referring to the renowned Urdu poet Firaq Saheb. We also know him as Firaq Gorakhpuri.'

'Correct.'

'But sir, he was neither a singer nor a qawwal. He wrote poetry in Urdu and recited them in Mushairas. He won the Jnanpith, the highest literary award of the nation.'

'Okay, okay. Happy you know these things. But talk less. What about your father?'

'He was employed as an auditor-cum-accountant in a private shop.'

'An auditor in a private shop. And accountant too. Beautiful but rare combination indeed. Is he retired now? Normally, employees of petty shopkeepers don't retire.'

'They may not retire but they can be dismissed any time for no substantive reasons. They don't have the protection people have in government. My father was sacked for some fuzziness in the accounts, a charge that he has denied for the longest time.'

'And have this lesson from me. Here once competent authorities frame charges, rest assured they will be proven. Come what may. Matter of honour, you know. In the services, precedence is used to fuck either side whichever way pleases the competent authorities. So avoid controversies. But you just told me...'

'Of accounts and audit.'

'You are too young. You don't have an idea of how accounts are compiled.'

'Sir.'

'Listen. Fuzziness. Bullshit. That's the beauty. That makes one a great accountant. My boss used to say, "Accomplished accountants are ones who know more of audit than accounts and that ensures only fuzziness." Unfortunately, my boss died in harness. He was tracking classification and was found dead in his chair with his pen at rest on a thick volume of file named "Monthly Accounts". That is what fuzziness in accounts all about.'

'Sir.'

'You can follow nothing. You can…,' before he could complete, the buzzer of his phone made a bee-like sound. I was amazed—phones made music. I heard someone telling him something and then he said, full authority on display, 'Tell him to try it later, say late evening, as I am busy now.' He kept the receiver down. Used the buzzer again, 'Tell him, I am awfully busy.'

Third cardinal principle: words should be carefully selected to have the intended impact. Those failing in this art of precision are doomed to suffer incivility of the high order.

I felt emboldened.

'Sir, I seek your kind permission to share one of my problems.'

'Hmm, but quick please,' he started looking at his wrist watch as he completed the sentence.

The fourth cardinal principle: when you anticipate a problem, behave like a busybody. Just look the other way, you know. And leave everything else to your deputy, if you are first-in-command. But if you are second-in-command, then start yelling at your immediate subordinates.

'I have a slight problem, sir. I suffer from insomnia.'

'Then you have a medical problem and you have just entered the hierarchy. Anyway, consult a doctor. Preferably a psychiatrist. Manju, my PA will assist you. Now leave my room. Others are waiting outside.'

'My problem will be greatly solved if the congestion in the room is eased,' I persisted. I knew it was risky.

'What congestion? You are comfortably placed in the hostel.'

'Nine in one.'

'Not clear. Don't try to set riddles. Only those in the higher echelons can set riddles and get away with them.'

'We are nine persons in one room.'

'Which room is it?'

'Room number twenty-eight.'

'It's a very big room. I think you have an attached room too.'

'Not much space sir. Nine persons in one room. One commode. Two buckets. One medium, one big. One plastic mug. Medium-sized. One small Lifebuoy soap, red, used by all nine. And scarcity of water every time.'

'Well, let me see what best I can do but that will only be much later. At present, stay with what you have.' The second-in-command sounds like a wise philosopher.

'Sir, S.A. has been given a single room. Can't I get one too?' I am determined to seek a solution.

'Oh. Okay. But young man, you know S.A. is the topper of the batch. We go by seniority.'

'Sir, is he from Italy? He is so fair and speaks shreshtha English.'

'Oh no. It's not shreshtha English, it is chaste English. Pronounce words correctly. Try at least. You are really from the cow belt. Not all fair coloured fellows are from Italy. Don't generalize everything. Your father was an auditor and you must know this tribe of auditors are past masters at generalizing things. You have a long way to go, boy.' Then he gave some surreptitious signal to his PA. This resulted in a knock, a gentle one, and the entry of a sufficiently cute looking girl. I noted cautiously second-in-command's glance travelling from top to bottom, scrutinizing her inch by inch. His glance halted at places more attractive than others. I did not fail to note a strange type of coarseness in her voice. And as I was lifting myself from the cushioned chair paving the way for the girl to occupy the chair, I heard him saying in a raised voice,

'Before you leave, let me tell you and you can take it as a word of caution. Knowing about your background, I am in no doubt that you have to put more than your best to acclimatize with the ethos of this institute. I am sympathetic but very tough. Even my seniors are shit-scared of me. Twenty years of seniority, you know. You will be under my personal scanner. And let me tell you one more thing. I have not taken very kindly to your complaints about accommodation. You have to understand collective ethos, commune living and the rigours of hard work. These are the pervading philosophies of this institute. And remember, I have put in twenty years of service. A word from me to those higher-up will be disastrous.' He concluded rather snappishly.

Yes, sir. May I go now, Sir?' I feel insulted when I find how the coarse-voiced girl is looking at me—wry and pathetic. I realized the meaning of what I had heard people often calling 'pangs in the heart'. But then I heard second-in-command's concluding murmurs, 'What a schizoid? As if there has ever been a dearth of schizoids here that one more has come.'

I leave the room—calm, agitated, composed, irritated, cool, and suffocated. I find myself no better than Jeremy Smith. Worse than him. Azorka might join later. Though not very worried, I foresee the aftermath.

The fifth cardinal principle: seniority is determined the moment you join and it determines what you will get till your superannuation. You become an indelible part of the list—a sanctum sanctorum which reigns supreme in caves of different shapes and forms.

Overall cardinal principle: to succeed, blindly follow the hackneyed accomplishments of those who matter, eulogize in abundance even when not needed. Also remember in hierarchies, precedence is cited to fuck those whom seniors don't like and also reward those whom they like. Hierarchical structures hinge on precedences. No harm in it but how a precedence is interpreted makes your life a success or a failure.

'May I sit, sir? The cute girl asks. As she spoke, second-in-command carefully watches her lips—full, stiff and gluey. 'Yes, of course you can. Your name is Gehna. Right.' His affection for her is noteworthy. What conversation occurred between the two thereafter became an untraceable part of history as I left the room and have no material to elaborate on.

∫

'Don't guzzle your dinner. The world is not going to fall apart,' T. Vilayati, the man with the moustache, occupying the chair next to the long-faced lady, said loudly, trying to draw my attention towards the manner in which I was having my meal.

'Who is this fellow? He hardly speaks.' It was now the long-faced lady R. Zameera's turn to speak, her voice, icy and soft. A cool predator. T. Vilayati adjusted his napkin. He was careful and smiling. A peon entered and handed over a tiny packet to T. Vilayati. I looked from the corner. The cover read—Bihari Zarda (Tobacco from Bihar).

'Seems a deviant personality.'

'Is it?'

'The chap is ruthlessly silent.'

'What an expression—ruthlessly silent.'

'Shameless, doesn't even respond.' They were speaking about me. Voice low, eyes twinkling, lips eager. I could hear them. For many eyes, my mere presence was an offence.

'But a guzzler.'

'May I have some curd?' I asked in a low voice, as low as possible. Another man, P. Chandrika was sitting in front, and talking fanatically, addressing the whole gathering without bothering much if someone was listening. He was eloquent and never devoid of energy. His neck moved in a peculiar rhythm—to and fro. Long-faced lady watched that, looked at me, found me watchful and smiled. With every word spoken, his neck would move to an angle ranging from forty-five to sixty degrees, and it would move as if it was resting on some spring-based element. Unconcerned about the spit flying out rapidly and in good quantity, sufficiently spoiling others' food, he busied himself. To me, he appeared to be a fellow afflicted with hyperactivity. Psychologists call it a hypersonic personality.

'Will you please pass on the bowl of curd?' I reiterated. I had a desire to leave this place early. These conversations on countless topics were irrelevant and lacked direction. This time the hyperactive man took pains to move the bowl towards me, but continued with his animated and unsolicited conversations.

The small doorway with no door, big enough to allow easy entry and exit to medium-sized persons with a height of 5 feet 7 inches or so, had a very important role to play in the prestigious institute. It connected the dining hall to the lounge where a hub of activities during late evenings was a routine occurrence. A highly heterogeneous group of individuals had gathered there and busied themselves in tasks each one of them considered to be of prime importance to others. Mixed voices, yells, whispers, loud talks, domineering summons, sound of music, some classical music, a western singer mouthing at the peak of her voice a song (all Greek and Latin to me), a newsreader reading Hindi news—all this was happening at the same time.

But of all the voices that could be heard, there was one that distinguished itself in terms of intensity and impact. 'Look that way, have you heard it? How the hell can this be allowed?' the man said, perhaps inadvertently, with a special stress on the words, 'Look that way'. None reacted; none was interested. If anyone was, it was lost in the din. There was a giggle though.

'Oh my Ghosh, there are hardly anne (any) good vegetarian

items in dinner,' the strange-voiced girl Gehna was protesting the menu but none joined her in her protests. She kept sipping the tomato soup sucking the abundantly swimming thick cream. It was as cold as curd and tasteless. It was neither sweet nor sour. In my mind it was like History of Economic Thought—frigid.

'All thoughts that make history are frigid thoughts,' I remembered my old, half-bearded teacher, Professor Ganguly voicing this every time before initiating his students into any topic on the subject. 'One day, this lousy Professor would make us frigid.' I told one of my friends. And got an immediate clarification from him. 'Only ladies can be frigid. Gentlemen are impotent.'

'Thus, if you believe Professor Ganguly, all historical thoughts are feminine in origin,' I retorted. Sometimes, I retort too.

The strange-voiced girl, for no fault of hers, caused in me an association of thoughts, thoughts I had almost forgotten. Was her voice not similar to that of Professor Ganguly? Her voice represented frigidity of economic thought.

'Look that way...,' the words came again. 'Hi-Hi-Hi-Hee-Heee,' the giggle again.

I was at a loss. What personalities I was to put up with. And for how long. The strange-voiced girl, the words 'Look that way...', the highly-talkative man spluttering his spit, the giggling girl—all of which led to a chaotic reservoir of noise, everyone talking aimlessly about everything under the sun, none interested in listening, intellectual inertia or dementia, flying Hi-His, Hello-Hellos, hallowed laughter. Bloody nonsense. I finished my dinner and while getting up thought of the ensuing ethos of coexistence.

CHAPTER 4

The Dream and Suicide

I am waking up or is it a bizarre hallucination? Am I in a delirium? All hallucinations are not bizarre. Hallucinations—cold and joyless or violent and rapturous are just like dreams but you see these when you are awake. Thinking about voices make them start up. But most of these have logic. You are hungry; you see food. You are dying of thirst; you see water. And you say hallucinations have no basis. This is bullshit. I have tried to figure them out. You too just think about it.

Not long ago, the powerful acousma clawed me in the company of those high calibre people and also in the company of the mornings I spent in the garden watching insects, bees and honeybees hovering around flowers of different colours—hues colouring my imagination. I started thinking as to what led poet Jules Renard say of a butterfly, 'this love letter, folded in two, is looking for a flowery address'. Marcel Proust found in his interpretation of this line both the conceit and the truth substituting one for the other. He spotted the butterflies flitting intuitively from flower to flower, from enquiry to enquiry which must have proved to be a fiasco ordained to end as a means of escape. It is contrary to what Proust said earlier praising Renard for fathoming a sensation and seizing the whole truth. I am afraid, for me, the sensation may stir another round of sensation—each with a deeper purpose, deeper sense, deeper articulation of the same message—the tentativeness of the search and the enquiry.

Sometimes thoughts on suicide reverberate inside me, not of committing it but it makes me think of life. The succeeding moments make preceding ones redundant—last night, I slept at eleven o' clock and when I got up it was nine of the same night. Amazing, but I didn't feel like that. Time had worked itself backwards—it had walked backwards as memory moves backwards and gives me undesirable connections. In travelling backwards, I moved past my connections, the entities that engulf me on my being in a state of fugitiveness. I was and still am a fugitive. Will always be. I am thinking of this actress who had taken her own life; the nation stood devastated at the news of this incident. She is going to appear in my dreams too.

Did I ever have any suicidal thoughts? Is suicide not required to be one with oneself? The shy philosopher went where his entire ilk ultimately goes leaving the rest with a shivering stillness. Life's ambivalence admits of no such motives.

Then there was the painting in my dreams. I looked deeply at it. A not too graphic description of the figure but the background extended it beyond itself—the wide edges, angles, contours—no, none of these never were, but something similar to them, something similar which I found difficult, at the moment, to cling on to, to search for the words that would describe that 'something similar' candidly enough, to enable me to understand them. I slept for three hours and lo and behold the haze had vanished—the painting was much clearer now, much more absorbing than when I, with my eyes open and brain alert, had looked at it. The secret of clarity lay in my sleep: deep sleep. It was a white world; as white as snow that had just fallen—thick layers of snow scattered all over—the earth was off-white, the dead had just been buried. None would rise from the grave. There were crows flying silently in the sky. Silence sheltered itself in whitened silence. My sleep crawled on, undisturbed—so unusual. Meaning had started dawning upon me and as I looked at the painting, its meaning was melting with my existence. My sleep gave me a new understanding of life which like that painting, once upon a time, stood as meaningless as the painting with undecipherable contours.

A white world was no world—it was a snowy world which would ultimately melt away. Was then, the young actress trying to reign in that white world? Did this white world suck her? White had its own naturalness. Snow…snow…and snow—unleashing fluctuations. I heard the loud laughter—someone laughed. Did you hear it? No? Try and hear it again? No? I went to look there— there was nothing. I was still in deep sleep. This midnight would draw whatever I missed all along. Did I not miss the edges, the overhangs, the angles, the contours?

My dreams, at times, get enraged—these probe my mind but like things ephemeral buried beneath the layers of snow—I mean that painting—my dreams never cross me. Obscurely dawned the occurrences but I was in deep slumber. Imperceptibility was supreme; I was relishing my confabulations. The dead actress was nowhere in sight. But the painting was. Perhaps under snow— mounds and mounds of snow—or walking or seeminly standing. But she seemed to be walking alone. One walks alone when in dire straits. All alone. Life gives one this humble lesson. And you still live and live daringly. Multiple images continued jarring against each other as I fixated my eyes more closely on the snow-laden blank spaces: opalescent. The images streaked, danced and above all dodged but without any movements and vibrations. No real happenings. Spaces were vacuums resisting any possible perception. It was looking like a traveller would suddenly emerge from this vacuum and ask the dead actress to accompany him. He did indeed come and she went along. But stay for a while, I have not finished as yet. I have yet to make a foray into the lively monologue in her mind.

A very old, tall and unruly man was reading loudly from Edgar Poe's poem 'Al Aaraaf':

> Within the centre of that hall to breathe,
> She paused and panted, Zanthe! all beneath,
> The fairy light that kiss'd her golden hair
> And long'd to rest, yet could but sparkle there.

It was an animated reading though in a voice blurred and hoary—adding an inflection, resignation, and self-weariness. He seemed to be having great trouble standing straight. He could hardly breathe normally. It seemed his passion for poetry had punctured his lungs considerably. But he had secured a permanent place on the snowed canvas. Incidentally, both his hands were tied at the back and very surprisingly, he never felt uncomfortable even momentarily. Instead he waved both his hands with equal ease and zeal that matched the best orators naturally inclined towards gesturing—using their hands in sync with their tongue as they are hell-bent on impacting a docile and helpless audience.

Tied hands struggling to be untied. It was my dream—underway. Imagination has a basis; it propels itself by that. Suicide is like an unclear photograph—the more you look into it, the more confused you will emerge. No animal ever commits suicide. Nor do objects supposedly possessing no life—tables, chairs, lamp posts, office buildings, letters we write. As you ward off the unclear elements, you see the photograph more vividly—you see patterns within patterns and you see how turbulent a mind can be which a face never reflects. The audience the lanky old poet had by any normal standard, was a captive one but there was only one chair with invisible legs. The actress sat on it, casually, as if nothing of any consequence was happening around her. Her mind seemed obsessed with things I could never lay my hands on. Emerald light—off and on—on and off. The ruins in her frozen mind must be howling—her image, naked and flat fluted beside her.

'Enough has happened. I am cussed now. Mental myopia has ruled me—days have become nights; nights, days. Where do I feature in your scheme of things? My skin is dead. It has lost its sheen. You have given me only voids. All through I sought you: my death. All through I have lived just to seek you. I have clear intent. I will go, very early, earlier, much earlier,' she proclaimed. There was a long pause. At least I heard nothing though she moved here and there in complete silence; sometimes her lips murmured something but nothing could be heard. My ears grew insensitive. She stirred again, 'I experience an inner turmoil; I want to meet my metamorphosis, and complete it. That bare one hour does not cheat me. I am too near. I have wronged none; I have crossed none. I cherish no oceanic oneness with you. I cherish no seduction from you. I want that one moment—the single moment that freezes me out there—the end of the horizon.' Recrudescence of silence. I was caught unawares. The day that began with silence ended gracefully with greater silence. Not a single visitor. But I heard that luring laughter—luring me away from everything but my repugnance. Like a toad, I waited but nothing happened. But did I expect anything to occur? This place is worth no occurrence. Wavering curtains touching each other as if in consolation. 'Macro temporal voids—come and gulp me,' she said to herself.

∽

Six hours back, it was 1.30 past midnight and perhaps an airplane flying at an unknown distance, far off in the sky sent the waves of its sound to me. It was so far-fetched as to give no dreams at all. I prefer nights sans dreams; dreams enjoy a battered life when they stand detached from hypersensitivities that, of late, have engulfed me. I start thinking in terms of my limping down to a world of regaled monument: a bizarre monument at cross purposes with its own ignominy. There are times when images repeat themselves without any one of them flying away from me. I try to wake up from the seizing but find the conscious power, almost the forgotten one, dying. I feel the seizing; wake up from it without even knowing where my next steps will take me. A nonplussed man, needing someone near me, someone very close to me who can hear the voices oozing from my ears, from the innards of my brains. Rail tracks are empty and the moon is nothing but a vibration of its own. The absent hands of thought torment me as I am pitted slowly against a plain emotionless desert. There is no sand. Emotions are worse than sand. Sand falls from one's hands but emotions always keep sticking to you. Unlike sand they never leave one's hands tempting one to stay awake to dreamless and faultless stories. Helpless hands unable to wreck the webs of emotions write palpably.

∽

I realize the presence of my uncle; his sudden presence telling me that life exists. I feel in his voice a scintillating sensation: the sound of the dirge which he wished he could have sung but could not. The sound of that dirge has gathered—such voices give life to the ink that pens stories.

Where does this dream take me? Dawn but that was not peaceful. The dream content is on the walls of my mind. That painting like the dream content seems to be conjuring up the light and atmosphere of a world that is not natural. But the mist has not evaporated completely. Once it does and I hope it will soon, I can afford to reread the dream, know the actress and find the place in which the painting hangs. Till then, anguish remains.

CHAPTER 5

On Sex and Sensuality

Stories, often times, can be veiled. Lamentably, heart's greatest anarchy is that it beats and continues to beat until you are dead. Corollary to that is: pangs and revitalized pangs of gloom make it beat more clearly and more logically. When my six-and-a-half feet red jacket-wearing friend and I met in December 2016 after a long time, he engaged me in remembrance of things past, inter alia underlying the importance of 'forties' and 'fifties' in life thus: 'Forties and fifties are naughty, KK.' By 2016, I had crossed fifty-six and was heading towards fifty-seven but now let me confer about the period of upheavals plaguing my life for three years beginning with 2012.

∽

Carla D., 45, the photographer from UK, settled in Malta.

Seventy-eight years after his death, Sigmund Freud still holds much fascination for ladies. Otherwise why would Carla D., my esteemed friend, tell me, 'You know Sigmund Freud once said: "What does a woman want?"' My friend thought he should have come up with a philosophy saying, 'Why do men always misunderstand women?' Okay. Then she left the choice of going either way entirely to me. She didn't even know what wrong she had done. Or why I was normally in a huff, but if that was the way I wanted it, then so be it. Perhaps I would stop letting her deter me and the philosophy of other creators and take time to enlighten her from my own wise philosophy of life about what, she as a woman, had done to upset or anger me? Ignoring her was rather rude and it irritated her. 'Women need to say no more. Even without saying anything a woman can convey enough. If you don't understand that, well then, anything is possible. I hope, KK you understand what is going on with me now?' Her parting words carried a sense of caution.

∽

8.30 a.m. The otherwise unused landline jerked me. It rang. I did not need it but it rang. Many times you don't need things but they force themselves upon you augmenting your perplexities. I was in no mood to pick it up and it stopped ringing, thankfully. I felt relieved as if spared of an imminent disaster. I continued to be seated on the chair endeavouring to ward off the irritation that follows after a telephone has rung for a long time—that disturbed lull. I wanted it to evaporate as fast as possible. But exactly at 8.45 a.m. the nasty thing waved again. I thought the best remedy to fight the bull was to take it by its horns. I moved hastily towards the telephone, lifted the receiver and heard a very feeble 'Hello. Morning my dearest KK'—her voice was thin and meek as if some unknown little force was carrying it to my ears. I knew it was her and I knew it too that she would be pouring out all her explanations about my indifference towards her. She had a curious feeling that she was losing me to someone as if I were a commodity and my possessor would greatly profit from that. That was the precise might of love or even platonic love.

I let her speak. 'Please be brief. I am tired and don't want to continue,' I said.

'I should clear my doubts. I guess I have no self-confidence left in myself. Especially my voice. It is becoming very negative of my whole being...' Then a pause ensued for thirty seconds or a bit more; she seemed to be having some sort of hesitation but then she continued, 'I'd like to know what you do in your leisure and how you think. Your mind intrigues me, in fact, your whole being does. I admire all you do and feel. I think you intoxicate me.'

'I feel fed up,' I muttered as if there was no better thing to say in response.

'No, no dear, not fed up. Never feel fed up. You should always bother me. One thing. Never dismiss someone who loves you. And I am happy you like my photos, yet I hope you would like some of my updates sometimes too. I take all the time, depending on my mood. I am not good with photographs of me in company of someone or sitting and posing. I prefer to be alone and look at my own self-confidence. In fact, I detest people coming near me with a camera.' There was a long pause at the other end and then she said, 'That way I am relaxed, I don't feel worthless then,' she stressed last ten words. Or eleven words maybe.

She continued, 'I miss you. It has been a very peaceful week for me of solitude. All here had gone away to the islands. So it was nice to be here with just me. I wish I could live all by myself. I have realized I can cope with life better, doing this. All alone.'

I realized there could be music when you do nothing else, but listen.

'I wish to travel. By myself. Just to be me. Find who I truly am. There is a world out there with people I've not met that I wish to see. You know I have not met you...'

'Can we talk later?' I said, this time emphatically, but she had her own designs.

'This year. I think it is time this year to see about getting a book published. I feel more confident writing now. And in my older poems, I look back and see so many mistakes I need to edit. The lady publisher, that woman is so self-indulging—she irritates me; her ego is insulting, to say the least. She phoned me here at home once. Even on the phone she irritated me.'

I was least interested in her narrations but sometimes you blame yourself for your helplessness. 'Can we talk later?' feebly mouthed words had no nuisance value but I felt she was reaching the end.

'You, you fill me. You know you are inside my veins. You should know it. Forgive though my stupid ways. My adverse nonsense. It is really unforgiving.'

'I will talk more later. It hasn't been long since I have woken up. I need to eat, drink and just spend time browsing a little before the day starts. I hug you. I love you. I need you. There, trust in what I say.' Then, I kept the receiver down.

∽

She was complex.

Now the question is this. It has taken turmoil, spiteful thoughts and words that are untrue on my part. Now when I am tired of sitting and feeling sad, I think and ask myself, 'Does anyone think the world of me and admire all that I do in everything?'

Carla D. said one day, 'I need your words; not your silence. I confess your words give me responses, opening up sharable things. KK, are you one with me?'

I remember sending this poem to her:

Inauspicious blanket of a multitude,
I feel surrounded; hibernating shapes,
A transcendent noise spread in its vastness;
Another day without dawn—thy love I wouldn't have,
I feel cold—outside my ecstasy stands frozen.

She was insistent on my explaining to her what I meant by the poem I sent her. I obliged. Spontaneity gives a poem a meaning which is attached to the happenings at that particular moment in the mind of the poet. When that moment is over and the verse is written, nothing stays back with the poet. Unfortunately, I am not one of those who keep explaining the inner meanings of their poems to equally zealous listeners. A poem may be rubbish for many but to a particular reader it may be a piece worth merit. For me, once I finish a poem, I find it dead at least for that particular point in time and on second reading, months or even years later, I find something to think over. In the one I sent her, the fourth line is the crux of the poem with the first three lines leading to the fourth and fifth epitomizing the end. With words like 'blanket', 'multitude', 'surrounded', 'hibernating', 'noise', 'vastness', 'day', 'dawn', 'cold', 'frozen'—I have brought together the meaning which I would have preferred stay concealed. Next, a reader creates his own world of thoughts and ideas after reading a poem: what really matters is his own personality, value system, motivational pattern, perception and above all, intellect. 'Oh, my God! What an explanation? Took my breath away,' her response came late at night.

∫

A week goes by.

A response made its way addressing me as 'My Dear Man'. The poem the response contained was passionate and revealing of the inner craving on her part to reach for me, touch me, embrace me in totality. I felt it deeply, I was almost one with her in her ecstasy, her offering of herself, in body and being, to me, and in return I was ready to offer her me and mine.

> When you sit at night in solace and
> you feel an ache rising...
> when your pulse fastens your heartbeat and

> your breathing desires to sip the wetness
> hidden behind that smile...
> feed me your deepest thoughts in words...
> Do it... It is just you and I in your solitude...
> Patience is a virtue
> A price—my value is worth every aching minute.
>
> Remember KK, I suffer from mental illness. I am unpredictable. But remember one more thing, my virginity stays unvisited thus far. A precious gift, dear...

I read the poem many times and was aghast at the pith and marrow of her creative faculty. A feeling of completeness overwhelmed me. Marvelling at the might of the poem, I made my last drink—the usual 50 ml raised to 100 ml. It was hard. There was a feeling of excitement in the offing.

*

My approach towards her was straight, sans remorse, and in tune with my views about her.

'You have filled me with a gusto of inexplicable nature.'

Carla D. read my words again and could not sleep. She loved that description, 'Gusto of inexplicable nature'. She felt it could make a very good title for a poem, 'Bewitched'. My poetry had cast a spell on her from day one. 'You are mystical, pure indulgence, a wonderful soul, my admiration is so high, and sometimes I think I should explode'—were her initial admissions. It was a great pleasure for her to have met such a man who had wisdom and who grasped life like she did. She had read another poem of mine—'An Evening'—its last four lines:

> The shadowy nymphs irked me off and on, an unending story/ like a lily drowning selflessly in a watery pond of tearless tears./ My chivalry gazed at undecorated asymmetries of the

evening/ while her icy crookedness tantalized the eloquence of ageless seers',

She said, 'I agree these thoughts can imprison us heavily...but what is life without these thoughts from time to time...on a lonely evening or an evening when one cannot sleep...'

My continued acquaintance with her helped bring newer dimensions of her life to the fore. A loner in life, she had lots to say on that, but in reality she claimed to be very quiet, shy and kept to herself. 'Socially dysfunctional. You understand,' she used to say. But she was happy to be so and had great appreciation for someone like me who she thought gave so much love to the many happenings in life, and put in beautiful words for an innocent like herself to witness the feelings those happenings encouraged. She was infatuated with my words. My poetry and interests took her deeper into a place where she could wait for my next words to appear. She appreciated my confidence with words. She was glad she did not offend me but she worried.

'Loneliness makes a great poet and thinker. I have many thoughts but I have never put pen to paper. I have no self-confidence.'

She dreamed away her life in her own world, enjoying, meeting new people from around the world. She became withdrawn day after day. She had a hidden sadness maybe no one could see in her photos. She felt glad—'I think last winter, yeah correct, you saw "dazzling splendour" in my photos. I was amazed at your quoting Cowper.' That photo was taken during a point in time in her life when she was at her lowest ebb, suffered from not eating, had withdrawn from life in such a deep sense that she could barely hang on to her life.

'Life is very trying. KK, you should know it.'

A few days back, very different words came from her.

> My mind feels all the nonsense and I get sad. I love my own time and research. My mind teaches me a lot of things always… I am a curious one wanting to know what life and art offer'

> For you:
> I hide myself within my flower,
> That wearing on your breast,
> You, unsuspecting, wear me too—
> And angels know the rest.
> I hide myself within my flower,
> That, fading from your vase,
> You, unsuspecting, feel for me
> Almost a loneliness.

Emily Dickinson is Carla D.'s favourite poet.

✧

'Why are persons like you and me always sad?' I confronted her.

'Because we channel other people's feelings? Because we both have lives that aren't full? Because having love in life and wanting to share in the flesh every day and the feeling thereof are sometimes unbearable and unnecessary. I wish everyday my mother hadn't given birth to me. We all have bad days. We're all lonely, if only we'd admit it.'

And early this morning, she conveyed to me she would give anything to be hugged and lived properly in the flesh. And she would wait.

She found the lines: 'Puzzles/sit down, awaken/beside me/as silences pile up/vaguely everywhere' from the poem that I had sent her perfect in every sense of the word. She did not want to change it at all.

'I speak from a true heart. I have the privilege to meet you in this very trying world we live. Don't change it KK. It overwhelms my heart and soul; it seeps deep into my heart and you know that too. You, for me, are something really extraordinarily perfect. Each time I read your poems, I feel comfortably numb, and for some unknown reason, tears. Please, these lines from the poem are perfect. But if it helps, if you are thinking something needs to be changed then there is just one word I dislike but this is my choice—"vaguely". Perhaps "nebulously" you can use. Maybe I misunderstood? Or any word but "vaguely", but I truly love this poem; it is perfect. Now, I will confuse you I suspect.'

Her love for me kept her sane: 'Thinking of you is sanity'. She sat in her bedroom chair some nights, in the middle of nights when awake, looking out of her window and wondering what I might be engrossed in, what I was thinking, how my day had been, if I ever thought of her. 'Probably not. But never mind. I don't ask you to, but allow me to think of you, it's a blessing that one wishes to keep forever. I am your pest in life, I know it.' When she felt my low morale and sadness which she could feel through exchanges, it made her want to come and hug me. 'Is that wrong of me? Am I wrong in wanting to hug you and wishing to know your thoughts?' She never thought otherwise. She longed to know my thoughts.

'One day, you will relax in my company here; and I am waiting KK.'

She had all the excuses for her discussing issues in her life. She was happy to learn that I had decided to be more open and personal with her now and how I could help her with my mind. She could not undo the past of her life. No one could. We can learn to deal with our bad dreams in some way or another, or lock these up in the back of our minds and suppress them. 'These things happen to us all, the best way you can help is to always be more personal and open. My goodness, if we, after all this time, cannot be direct and personal to each other, something is wrong.' She complimented me for my breakthrough of being a slight extrovert for some time now but had her apprehensions, 'Don't go stepping back into your being—an introvert completely. This new part of you that you have opened is a new beginning. At least for me.'

Then, Carla D. addressed me as her 'angel'.

∽

Was that a mistake? Did I write it inadvertently? In retrospect, I wouldn't have had an inkling of its consequences. This was what I wrote, 'I am really enamoured by you and find myself incapable of responding.' I thought my courtesies dictated at least one response from her.

She first attributed her contemplation that consumed her 'entire' afternoon to the word 'enamoured'. 'Now I have spent all afternoon contemplating your words—So…when you write "enamoured"…in what context are we speaking? Inspired? Enchanted? Captivated? Besotted? Crazy about? Sorry but I must ask…I am curious as usual? Also, incapable—why so? Because you are "unable" to? Not receptive to the idea of responding? Not being in a state of mind to respond? Feeling helpless to respond? Not admitting? Incapable of feeling empathy to my words?' She continued with her questions, 'Now when you have time, tell me into which category are you putting "enamoured" and "incapable". I know what they mean, but so many definitions and mostly the same confuse me. You know what I mean. I have a very curious mind and I always need answers.'

'Don't be afraid since you are an intelligent man. Come on, tell me what category are we speaking here? Help me understand your mind a little more, help me understand what it is that makes you crazy about me, if I am correct in saying so. And be honest of why you don't respond at times. In fact, most of the times. I have many guesses and some keep coming back to me but I would prefer to know your explanation. Come on my dearest friend, let's play with words. Give me a philosophical and detailed view of me. How they make you feel exactly and your response? I am asking you to participate. You like words, so do not be shy.'

And she changed the mode of addressing me as 'my sweetheart'.

∫

She spoke about her being audacious and vibrant but complained how the past year had sunk her deep. Her aim for the next year was to get back to what she truly was, and to find out what was vibrant for her—this was her New Year wish, no matter what happened. She had decided, 'Life is too short to be so sunk. I am only mid-forties. I should not be melancholic.' Then she came to the main issue, 'I also do not want any problems between us KK. It is my fault, all those tantrums of mine, entirely my doing and I am really regretful of my behaviour. I pretend to be jolly, but it's hard to smile all the time. I had so many tears today for you because I miss you, your thoughts, presence here, there. I do not need to say anything more; you know already what I think of you.'

She was trying really, really hard to focus on a poem, you know, like literary things; she really was. But then she told me, 'When you are silent, my mind goes numb. Then I am so guilty in my heart of hurting your feelings and being so cruel and ungracious towards you. How can I ever forgive myself? It just happened, unplanned. I write things, before my mind clicks and tells me how stupid I really am. I don't think first that's my problem. I really do not want to lose you, or have you get so tired of me, you will just end up ignoring me forever. I really have to think now. What you do is your life; I have no right to complain of your choices.'

'So will I...from now on.'

⌇

Carla D. was sick of people and their deliberate nonsense and expectations that made her feel like she was nothing. She knew she was not afraid to express her emotions but there was confusion or illusion—her heart and soul knew. She wondered how she could write of her love and adoration in handwritten words to me, when she had no idea of who would see her letter. Her confessions were logical. She kept writing and scribbling out her words and got nervous to send a letter felt from the bottom of her heart. For one she had no idea who else's eyes might see her words. That was not all. She had yet another doubt: if I was really interested in her heartfelt words? One part of her said 'yes'. The other part was nervous and curious.

'The most beautiful splendour is unknown, and this lady who is strange, falls in love with that splendour, I mean you—KK.'

She was candid. Love is all about being candid in relationships. But her expectations demanded from me an attitude of not being shy to her. She promised she would never remove me from her life. Her heart would never let her. She was afraid her words would put me off; make me silent. She had reasons for her fears.

'I feel I annoy you. When you are silent with me, I panic. I have little insanities. We all have, we would not be human otherwise. It is silence, and in truth, it makes my mind crazy. I mean that in a warm sense... I know you relish me...as do I. I don't need to say, you know me better than I know myself... I crave words from you. I am like you, I do not like to cause pain to people, unless truly necessary...and if ever I do cause them pain, I hope it is accepted with full understanding.'

She was being sagacious.

⌇

Beauty and intelligence—she knew I loved both. But what of the inner want, the desire? Not just any normal desire. But that warmth she felt of me, 'You know I am on fire inside.' Still, she wondered if I wished to hold her close with a depth that wanted to embrace her very existence, her mind. 'Let me reach the ecstasy hidden in you, waiting to disperse and merge.' She relished the love to lose herself in a passionate type of pain. It was a kind of lust: a giving of all that sweetness that poured from the very soul of desire. 'I know your mind. I know your desires. I crave to know these more. I know you have so much fire you wish to bequeath in words.' My holding back surprised her. 'Let me taste you through your words and thoughts. I am real with my dark painful lust… Your whole existence has filled me. It is more than just love. It is beyond your intelligence, your words give me all what I have craved for my whole adulthood. Demand from me… I am not asking for the moon.'

'Moon amidst fire,' was my response, but there was no further reaction from her.

Her gloomy face was before me, 'I am sincere, honest, sensitive…a woman of substance, strong, fiery, and straight to the point, holding no grudges,' she described herself and told me she was not angry but annoyed and dismayed wondering why I was saying one thing and doing another. 'I am all hot air as you know. You know these damn literary magazines: half [of them] do not have any essence and this editor, God knows why he is so rude, a pompous fool like everyone in this country. They write things—boring and rubbish.'

She found editors no better than twits; usually writers put up with them and use them. In the literary world, everyone uses everyone else; it is the way to go forward. You have to bite your lip and put up with their bad manners. But they have their uses. She wrote, 'Tired of losing myself. Well famous women writers feel that way. It's perfectly natural. Some people believe they need someone in their lives to feed the passion of their creativity. But that's not true. Write dear, of your sins for example. Your loves. Write of your life, what surrounds you. You have much in India to write about. Such a beautiful country. You've love in your heart. Women are sorcery. I think those times are long past when poets talked of women. So much more to see and feel. But write of the sins you have so beautifully perfected.'

∫

Carla D. was very natural.

'Can you imagine the two of us in the same room? We'd be at loggerheads night and day. Don't you also know that is a sign of true friendship?'

Then, a beautiful symmetry of 'I':

'Dear KK,

I make many mistakes in my stupid split moment decisions and some I do out of spite.

I think the world of you;

I have love in heart for you;

I think your job is remarkable;

I think your writing is the best contemporary poetry;

I miss you so much, it is breaking my heart inside, now feeling empty;

I am a fool swayed by nonsense.'

∫

It was 4.30 a.m. and I was thinking about her. Sometimes I wonder why it is so that two persons at such far-off places tend to feel one with each other. My answer is because they have the same mental wavelength—they meet, embrace each other, through that wavelength. Your appreciation for my poetry is indeed encouraging.

You mean each and every word you pen. When I put down what I thought of you, I never thought it will take us to those words we might not have even thought of. I get puzzled when I see in face stories of lost hopes, lost dreams and deprivations. But then these make a person a perfect human being. Deprivations have added lustre to you. You have simply blossomed. In you I get succour; in you I get what sails me through my literary journey. You are a mix of three graces—beauty, grace and gentleness. I rejoice in you as much as I miss you.

⁂

Carla D. opined about herself, 'I am the type of person who would give anything to anyone, I have a generous heart, and kindness comes naturally. You are more than any words can explain. You have my little mind constantly analysing everything now.'

A dangerous augury. So I thought.

⁂

Was it troubling to be drawn towards her? Attraction!

'If I were able to take you in my arms and embrace you with all the warmth and passion, believe me, KK, you would not be able to breathe another day without craving for more. Let me be plain with you,' she had told me this long time back. She was passionate, aroused by my speaking openly, by my photos. 'Your saffron/mustard shirt lightens your face with a certain glow—ambient. It gives an ambience of hidden seduction. A quality that reminds me of sweet jasmine and hidden spices enticing the palate of my passionate nature. I have a secretive lust, wanting of you KK.' She was in the midst of a storm that was waiting to explode.

'For you only on the blank last page I wrote a small poem I will send you later,' she wrote one day. Another beautiful symmetry of 'I', I said to myself.

'I just want to die KK.
I've had enough of this agonizing world.
I don't fit in it anymore.
I've no place in this world.
I can't find a place anymore that fits and makes me want to breathe.
I and life were not meant to be.'

It was yet to come closer to what you might call a fluorescent evening on the horizon but what Carla D. told me has stayed remarkably fresh in my mind. During lunch at a Delhi restaurant, that fifty-year-old, still very pretty, soft and marvellous lady capable of pleasing even the most misogynist of men said, 'I do know one thing. My poetry is far better than half the poetry you review. I know it's better than the Scottish laureate. I have a gift and you know that too. Though fame is not my scene, I will get published eventually now that I've begun to master flow and free verse. This is the first time I've thought of myself as a poet. You see I share only little. I keep all that in my file. My day will come. What do they say? Save the best for last. Now I'm being egotistical—wouldn't you say dear? I am not just a fake blonde. Or a woman. I have potential in many areas. One day, somebody might see that in me and not just in my appearance. Love to you dear, and no... I told you once, we would be forever friends. Love is always there. Ah ha, did you miss me? Is that why you kept away for so long? See my worth and we'll speak! You know two energies from opposite sides will always be there in each other's world. At least you should know that KK.'

I thought she had finished as I found her lost thinking—she was thinking of something: perhaps of the empty art of poetics or something else as I heard her last words—

'Write dear. Imagine your head in my lap, then write. You know relationships have a price tag.'

Tea and snacks arrived but Carla D. insisted for some wine.

⌒

'I was not angry, dear; I was dismayed trying to trace you but you did stay away. For how long. X number of months. So where have you been dear? Did you email? I didn't receive any. Well I haven't checked today, as yet. You seem a tad melancholic? I will come to you. You wrote the other day! Or... You come to me... I'm going to be fifty soon, I feel old and decrepit. Should I shoot myself soon? I missed you, where have you been hiding? I feel I'm in trouble at your end. You do know many men are baboons... yourself not included of course. When young, I used to travel up to London often on the train to see plays by Harold Pinter and others. *Equus* was my favourite play by Peter Shaffer. It's about a psychiatrist who was treating a young man with a pathological fascination for horses. Are you also fascinated with something? Some book, some movie, some pictures, some place or a woman: a woman who floods moonlight from horizon to horizon from room to room? Tell me; you know I respect honesty.'

I was listening patiently. What else could I have done?

⌒

One must admit that any man of intelligence who is shy will be weary and find a woman like my friend scary in all respects, especially when a woman like her starts to understand that man and his thinking. She thinks it is a wonderful thing to have a friend with a similar mind and who is somewhat shy. 'To have a man friend who is a little shy is like finding a true gem. I am a pain KK, and I know this. Don't worry of my antics.' She seemed wise. For the first time.

Her instincts of certain women here proved her right this afternoon; her theory was not wrong. She could see truths in the real character coming out of some. 'Huh...there is more to men than the exterior; the mind is the most attractive part.'

Oh well...she then ignored what she thought was ignorable and carried on regardless.

⁓

Madness is truth. It's when any creative man goes emotionally mad and dark that he can write sublime poetry. Do you get my drift? One has to feel hurt, pain, darkness, real deep love to the extremities of all to create words that drown the mind with beautiful poetry. Only then can words affect the mind of the reader. Desire—love—want. 'In your poetry, there is all—that's what makes you the perfect poet/writer... You suffer, feel, love, hate, desire and you have darkness. Some of the most intelligent people of this world are those who have not entered a university. Life gives us the skills and intelligence we have.'

Intelligence—I know what she implies.

⁓

Miss X, 41, a painter and writer from Goa: Sex is an exploration into intelligence.

> From the unseen horizon she descends—
> conveying to me multitudes a silence can have.

Though once she had admired the evocative power of words, she hardly uses words to establish her admiration for that power. I wonder about her nature which by and large lingers with me with its baffling propriety. Sometimes she would be pouring out her heart to me—her thoughts, her naiveties, but out of all these I could hardly lay my hands upon the basic thread that allowed my harmony with hers. The distance is enormous and absurd thoughts know no boundaries or should I be more specific, absurdity of love is a universal phenomenon. She knows it as much as I do.

Then one day I get a brief message, it is cryptic—'You are not my close friend.'

My plan to have intellectual connectivity with her dims and then vanishes slowly. I shudder at the thought of being in a lurch. Dusk is not far off, the sky is partly clouded with sporadic lightning here and there, and wind rushing past in great speed; it was most likely going to rain. There is the occasional barking of stray dogs too, tall trees swaying to the breeze—all this promises me a dark empire I would soon be lording over. I race up and down in that room of 15 by 15. Fed up and annoyed.

⌣

Wonderment was today's fruit. And why not? Did I ever expect it? Ask again. Yes. No. Never. But 6.50 in the morning did not augur well. A qubalistic message was in store: 'Will you please address me by my real name and not by the one you used?' What was it I had used? People call me KK. A shorter name—easy to connect, easy to associate. But the lady had a problem—a problem which she left unexplained but which I could sense the moment I read it and intensified version came through further probing of what was occurring inside my brain. Was I shocked or did I feel abased? Neither. Then exactly what? Believe me. And then came the laughter again, a milder one this time. Why none of the two can locate it? There is a laughter—I hear it; you apparently don't. Am I a dreamer—my own protagonist who enjoys false dimensions of life? The fan—not new and rusty was slow and its movement caused vibrations in the room, distractions of a certain type—undesirable and unruly as if a story is on with its never-ending struggle.

She could have told me instead. These ladies are of that type. They flower in secrecy; men guess why they behave so, like Madam. She was beguilingly silent keeping everything to herself; nothing revealed. Her cheeks, eyes, lips, chin—everything of value on her face I noticed from a distance and determined she was beautiful and innocent. Innocent beauty becomes a far cry, a distant dream. Innocence in beauty or beauty in innocence—whatever it may be, is lost with no hope of finding it. The next moment is an unwelcome one; the last one unworthy of any remembrance.

⌠

That disquieting night I had a disturbed sleep which was full of dreams. Sleeplessness, disturbances, suffocations and aberrations dominated my dreams. In it, she was standing, sitting, bending, talking, whispering, but not coming near, not accepting my kisses, not allowing me to embrace her, not holding my hands. The dreams carried the same intensity but did not reach the desired conclusions.

⌠

In a graver area where I feel more secured, more comfortable, I indulge in the luxury of my musings. Is it becoming a destructible part of my identity? My own thoughts? She has been in my thoughts for several months now. I feel her presence in me at times. I sense her, I smell her. I feel thirsty. I need some whiskey. It is chilly outside. The wind outside has liberty; nothing bars its movement. Trees, tall and strong, multi-storeyed skyscrapers, electricity poles, not to talk of human beings—nothing can hinder its freedom. I hear howling outside, howling of the wind as I move to a lighter room to fetch for myself a peg of whisky. A voice tells me—cover yourself, cover your face, it is ugly, it is unseeable, it is salacious.

⌠

I thought of initiating X into a larger literary world. I asked her to contribute a poem or two to a literary magazine of repute but she came out with an interesting question and it's that question which compels me to think, 'Very refreshing indeed. But, why me alone?' Those were her precise words. I would answer deriving partly from Marcel Brion who was reconnoitring the idea of time in James Joyce's work, 'All men are made similar by the nearly equal cadence of their heartbeats, but they are separated by the rhythms of their sensations or their thoughts. Only those walking at the same pace know each other.' The learned critic failed to add 'all women' forgetting that they too have heartbeats. But in retrospect, I find there is no answer. Certain questions/doubts have no answers. The universe decrees that way. Life is a nasty entity one lives through relating questions to answers. It seeks answers for a human being for his survival but oftentimes questions develop a tendency to stay unanswered. The beauty of life lies in the time when one confronts the vagueness of explored things which sometimes carry their pain garbed in pleasures. Whether I enjoy it or hate it, I could not possibly answer. 'Why' I cannot answer. 'Why' am I writing these today, years after the question was posed? Yet one more dimension. If I say that someday, someone else would be tackling this 'why' much after we have left this world, I will be the one hoodwinking myself. Very dense 'whys' we all are destined to live through. 'My sweet friend', my confession—that was how I once addressed X. We need, like Albert Camus said, 'virile silence and communion to solitary courage'.

After more than five years, I reread Albert Camus's *The Fall*. These lines arrest my attention when one talks of human behaviour:

> Tell me frankly, is there any excuse for that? There is one, but so wretched that I cannot dream of advancing it. In any

case, here it is: I have never been really able to believe that human affairs were serious matters.

And do you want to know the response that poured in.

'Don't think only you have read Camus. I read him when I was sixteen.'

I pondered when I read these lines if her response was a simple coincidence.

∽

X is very quiet. So am I. This is so glaring: masking the cauldron of ideas/perceptions/cognitions that make that person. X was quiet but was she so from inside? No. My guess might be misplaced. X's mind was seeped in her literary adroitness—it hid X but it tempted her to unravel, to unfold; a whole world was to be displayed—that enigmatic sleep might not sweep over her any longer. I will wake up and write. Did similar feelings not visit X? Did X not feel emboldened, emboldened enough to squawk at these muddle-headed creatures, 'Enough is enough; get lost. Let us have our say, now.' X did have these feelings. Her mind was in an unease undefined—it never comforted itself, it never located itself. The pain of consciousness was within; not outside. Why should we allow ourselves to have our throats slit for no fault of ours? The pain is to be displayed; courageously, candidly. I am not going to accept it any longer. I have suffered the pain of birth, my mother's pain, the pain of being a child who had everything but childhood, the pain of alienation, of suffocating solitude, of humiliation and of hypocrisy of those who matter the least for me but are my rulers. 'We are the custodians of thoughts: we ought to rule; not the thoughtless ones who rule us. Literature, of late, has become a façade. There are more flamboyant questions—questions that bring to fore our ability to enjoy life, to enjoy pleasure. Are those capable of thinking doomed to suffer?' X promised to get back.

⁂

I sat late last night confused, baffled. I thought to myself, was it time for winding up all sorts of socializing? The stupid place had been a bad omen to me from the start. I was not good in socializing with many. They were all ungracious at times. I would have preferred someone to be his/her true self than like half of those who always acted in such a saint-like manner. I sensed things. Instincts played a great part. My life was just endless; everything going wrong. So what was life trying to tell me? Nothing this year (2015) had gone right so far, especially in the first half. I was left stranded. Solo. No consolations. But I live life by instincts, daily with the flow. I do not live it based on others' views, entirely by my own. Same as my thoughts in poems, even though some may think of my writings as trash. I feel so guilty inside. I feel like I will just sink—then and there. It cannot be plainer than that. It was temper, nothing more. Blasting music in my ears last night, and deep thoughts early morning today made me realize it is time for me to take action and stick to it.

This time X was more forthcoming than earlier.

⁂

'A poem in trance'—I described it to X and recited it to her. This was a month back.

'Seductive power of words…you made me smile again…' X wrote back. Finally. Early morning.

⁂

The whole day I was filled with anxiety. She was becoming a source of great vexation for me. She had already become an inseparable part of my thoughts and that was painful. I went to the fridge;

there was no beer. I moved to the cupboard to be welcomed by five bottles of whiskey but all were empty. Here emptiness of life consisted of an unfulfilled desire—a desire that, I knew for certain, would never meet its finality. It will die a slow and painful death which I could see in the mirror but here the mirror was fixated in my brain and psyche. Obviousness, sometimes, takes your heart out of your body and still you live temporarily. I thought of her flashing beauty and in the evening, rains ensued, wildly raving wind—all dust inside the room—I was the paused moment in that room. Dust was my only memento. Rains continued descending; their intensity decreasing with time and ultimately ending in meagre drops. Like the hopes I once nurtured. At 9 p.m., the bell rang. I opened the door—dark night outside—a boy of ten, my maid's son, telling me, '*Amma aspatal mein hai; bachcha hone wala hai.*' (Mother is in the hospital. A child is expected.)

He left.

Darkness stinks.

∫

Did you just hear someone talking there? 'Let us go see who she is. Okay, you will not come, I will.' I went there again. A huge hollowness welcomed me. I came back.

My worries were of a different nature altogether. In my thinking of X she never mattered; it was myself in relation to her that was a source of my obsession. In my definition of her, I realized impending doom. You define someone and either you or that someone is doomed. The best relationships are already doomed relationships. You end before you begin or you never begin as you are already an end. Add to it silence—the greatest weapon of intriguing minds. She used that weapon, lethally. The whole day I was on the computer from ten in the morning to seven in the evening, thinking of X. She would come, post something, and I would read it. But nay reading it was never what I intended; what I really intended was completely unknown to me. Coated with mystery, I had yet to be initiated into it. X was there with all her smiles; her eyes and her lips drooping wine. A deadly combination that beauty is. Through her eyes she spoke to me, through her lips she peeped into mine, through herself she unsolved me. That was her, that was her beauty, her charisma.

My friend, these are moments of great exaltations for a man—when a woman wants him to understand her but in a way she dictates. Human anomalies are our greatest curse but we live happily with these. Again someone is talking. This time the voice is a little bit clearer. Oh, my goodness, you spoke at last. But where is that clearer voice? I went there. This time alone. That is all.

Life's all curves are for me. You heard a clearer voice but I didn't.

∽

My wait ended this morning. I was expecting it for over a month and it was to end today. X was thoroughly surprised to see an interview of mine that appeared in a magazine with the lady interviewer's photo on the page but she appreciated the woman who conducted it, describing her as 'very professional'. She expected me to imagine what the comment she had to make on it. She noticed how self-confident I was, and that she described as a good point. The strategy of the answers matched the map of my individual approach to writing. Of course, from her own point of view, she disagreed in many ways with many of my ideas.

'But it is your style and "le style c'est l'homme"', she said. 'It is a question of personality.' It was not possible for me to get the bigger picture of that. 'I see you. Here you are, in this moment in time and space (doesn't it sound great?).' It was high time for me to get out of the matrix in order to keep the creative process alive. Surely, the next step would be to keep writing. But, wait. It's not recommended to go on the same old track. She thought I shall have to make some changes. 'Let me share with you the map that I have in mind for you.' I found it interesting. What changes for the next stage: the next book? It must keep readers alive. What would I say about letting behind the people who have influenced me for the books so far? All the people I have in my mind as a source of inspiration are dead! They are really dead. The ideas that served me have been circulating and vibrating for a while at maximum capacity, and then taken over by other people who have taken their pattern by implanting their adaptations and transmutations to their territories. Just like me. But no more. These ideas carrying vapid material, after being alive for a considerable amount of time, have to come to an end of their sovereignty.

∽

'Psychology and philosophy are nothing but a world of borrowed wisdom,' X begins as aptly as ever.

I have to stop liking people that are now dead and gone. There are other interesting sources of inspiration, leading-edge people that have appeared in the meanwhile, at the end of the twentieth century and the beginning of the twenty-first. I have to stay in tune with my times, to move away from psychology and philosophy, a world of borrowed wisdom. Believe me, there are serious reasons. These two domains are bound to become only a vague and experimental pilot episode for our era. Yeah, how long would it take? Difficult to predict but I now feel it's just theory and only a scratch on a surface. In the meantime, incredible tours de force have been made in the field of evolution of thought. I must keep myself updated with the latest discoveries in neurosciences, genetics, physics and astrophysics. I must leave aside dead people and live along with the times. Today, her advice refuses to go—it calls for adjustments, imaginary adjustments. At least for now.

∽

The hair+
The eyes+
The cheeks+
The lips+
The chin=
Full Moon.
Blossoming, Smiling
...
Amid lightly dim night—
A poem for you. I wrote for you.

'Oh, my dear, unbelievable.' X was prompt.

∽

I told her that my next interview would not be far off. This particular interviewer had been on that job for the last fifteen years and had interviewed writers of eminence and amateur ones like me. But when the interview was over, the interviewer told me she found me a tough nut to crack. I didn't understand what she meant by it. I am very confident of myself—always, despite many odds going against me. I know sometimes a huge price will entail my confidence and that has actually happened. I have reposed my faith in my abilities and learning and so far they have stood by me.

The writers I mentioned are dead. But are their ideas dead too? I don't agree. Modern literature allures me no longer. Booker prize-winning novelists, including Indians, disinterest me; they inspire no confidence in me. You know what it takes to make these writers. I love the names I have taken—for me Marlow and Hazlitt are as important as Tagore and Yeats. X failed to understand that. It is the circumstances in society that create writers of all ilk—as long as circumstances that produce serious writers exist, their followers will exist and there will be similar writers. Similar situations produce similarly situated identities. There may be one or two around her, unable to cope with esoteric realities and the unreality of circumstances. But at the same time, I agreed with her: I have to move forward and I have really started moving forward, otherwise how come I mentioned her name. It was immediate.

∽

She expanded her explanation. In the past, she had never done so. Crippling expressions she put forth and had perhaps relished. I was not keen, yet it interested me. 'I appreciate everything you do: your work, writings, and analysis—all...' Had she not told me of this earlier? She had. Many times. But this time, something new, unexpected came: 'Your way of dealing with people. Please understand, I appreciate all these.' Bemusing though it was, it was freakishly intriguing. I was never good at dealing with human beings—the group dynamics; the human handling you know, who else can know better than your good self, sir. Fluttering of her eyelids. Dismaying flatness. Once again.

∽

I sent her a detailed mail expressing what I felt about her. Ten days have passed. No response from her. I have been livid. Unnecessarily sent it. I knew this lady's nature. She was beautiful, enchanting and highly intelligent but also arrogant and the no-nonsense kind. But, was she arrogant? Searched in Oxford Advanced Learner's

Dictionary. She was not as I read the meaning of that word. Then, serious, yes serious—very serious. Oh, okay. That would fit in. I told her: look, take this as friendly advice. I don't plan to inflict any wounds on you. Your beauty and intelligent bar that. My worst imagination would not run that high. What I am writing is friendly advice—an advice given by one friend to another. And I am no saint. So don't treat these as sermons. Not only that—I offered my apologies in advance if she feels I have hurt her feelings or sentiments or both.

It was after a lot of internal struggle—wavering between whether to send or not to send her the letter—I chose to take the risk and ultimately sent it to her. We had exchanged a few letters during the last few years. But this one compelled me to think about my endeavours several times.

These exchanges had enlightened me that I could feel beneath her 'too serious' nature and appearance lay an emotional and sensitive human being, perhaps seized with conflicts and associated frustrations that emanate from the outer world; a world full of buffoons and insincere people who unfortunately rule the roost and make the ball roll. In one such exchange, I let her know of my realization about how important a person she was. I cited Carl Rogers, the psychologist who spoke about maintaining, enhancing and actualizing one's personality vis-à-vis the rigidification of perceptions that sometimes call for adjustments and readjustments. We get shaken at times but the outer world stays unshaken. For a sensitive person it is indeed suffocating.

I let her know that apart from being a sensitive person, she was very intelligent and like people of her ilk, her sensitivities clashed with issues of moral values, personal growth and self-fulfilment that may be, more often than not, at cross purposes with the unacceptable realities of the outer world. This was what made her serious—very serious. To be serious was her, an intelligent person's prerogative. But it entailed a cost. I recommended to her Bertrand Russell's autobiography. It contained his correspondence with his contemporaries. Many contemporaries. In one of the letters Santayana wrote to Russell, I found this: 'People are not intelligent. It is very unreasonable to expect them to be so, and that is a fate my philosophy reconciled me to long ago.' Santayana, the philosopher, was known for his aloofness, detached personality, his spectatorial stance. I advised her to try and be a little 'less serious' since that would enable her to be much more at ease with herself. That way, I said to her, she would sense the realities or unrealities of the outer world as calming and soothing. Most of these are 'inferred' and this power of inferring belongs not to 'the common rut' but to the persons who after observing the outer world draw inferences from that observation.

'Are you not trying to reach and grip the same reconciliation? I think you are,' I asked her giving at the same time my answer: 'Herein lies the problem. We cannot help but infer and become sober. I hoped my sane advice will be appreciated.'

Months passed and one day she sent a reply, 'How funny? Anyway, I don't need an outsider's advice.'

∽

On the beach, one evening around seven, X tells me, 'I am in the worst possible position now.'

'Why?' I ask.

'I don't know. My brain power is decreasing. There are moments in my life that ruthlessly imprison me. I don't have an opportunity to neck out. I am facing testing times. What to do?'

'Use it. Use these testing moments. Don't forget, you are a painter. You write articles. For a creative person like you, these moments are both friends and enemies.' I try to give her solace. She seems obsessed; unable to listen and concentrate on my words.

'Can't think better for now. Losing my brain power.' X's face is not relaxed—something I would not like to see now. We don't meet so often. We met last, months back—the same beach.

'We cannot have "real joy". It eludes thinking persons and writers. Their thought processes clash with the utopia of real joy. But you create literature; you wallow in ideas. Try to get your first collection soon. Once you start working on it, you will start getting an inexplicable joy,' I tell her further.

'Do you have some idea about Sufism?' X buttonholes me. This sudden change of topic I accept, for I have to continue engaging her in conversation. After all, she rarely comes out of her silence.

'I am not well-versed in Sufism. I hear some Sufi songs by Indian singers,' I confess.

'These songs define a fascinating relationship between God and man,' X quips.

'Yes. Particularly in a monotheistic system where God is a historically conditioned expression of an inner experience. Is God not a conceptual expression of human experience, so prone to take the shape of an ideology?' I look at her face. It is as unrelaxed as it was when she came half an hour earlier.

'But can there be any danger of a mishmash of a concept and the experience it entails?' X comes closer; I hold her hand and find it soft—very soft.

'No. Remember the Zen Buddhists' saying, "the finger that points to the moon is not the moon"? God is without attributes, about whom no attributes of essence could be prophesied. Even in mysticism we find leanings towards independence and freedom of human beings and it includes freedom even from God. As a human being, we should have a concept of true independence, the ability to distinguish between rational and irrational authority, between idea and ideology and above all willingness to suffer for our convictions. Oneness with God is something I am never comfortable with.'

It's 8.30 now. X wishes to be dropped near her flat. I offer to drop her. She prefers to hire a cab. I look at her; she feels relaxed.

⌣

Wayward minds fall in love with the walls—the walls of our psyche, walls that are as imaginary as any mythical land with its opalescent blanks. In life, there is nothing but an allurement of being goaded into some comfortable level, if you seek that, away from your real life. But you never have the notion of fulfilment that comes when you live real life fully. Do I deal with real characters? Let me answer it. But before that, there ought to be an admission on my part. Let me admit that women, by and large, have eluded me in real life. Not that I got no opportunity. I missed them all, or better put—messed them all and messed them badly. But what I failed to achieve in life real, I realized in life unreal—it was a journey into what never existed, into the something masked in real imaginative perceptions. Of X's face, I thought of many comments—beautiful, just beautiful, ravishing, enchanting, mesmerizing, but then I spent three months to find the correct or most appropriate words. 'A poem in trance'. It was extreme luck or chance—the man who never even cared to look at a woman irrespective of her beauty chooses to fall in deep love with that 'poem in trance'. Nay, I correct myself—choose will be an inappropriately fixated word expressing something I never intend to be expressed. There was no choosing it. Her curiosity in me aroused curiosity about her in me. Curiosity met its counterpart. Curiosity is at the root of all love. Can I say so?

In meeting with my six-and-a-half-footer friend, I made my

confession as to how they or I became cosier to each other. He believed in the power of fantasy and exchanges and asked me, 'At least tell me who they are?' I see no point in the question. Seeing the triumph of incoherence, I am ever ready to meet life attired in a deeper mire of sorrow.

CHAPTER 6

The Behemothic Ethos

And the story continues. Salman Rushdie's great revelation in *East, West* that 'Most of us nowadays are sick' paves the way for me to ponder trivial things having lasting consequences. In my soliloquy, you—my six-and-a-half-footer friend—is the only company.

∾

'Fuck off you bastard, son of a bitch,' I heard a baritone voice, at least twice. Was it meant for me or anyone else in the motley crowd? None seemed to have heard it. Or taken note of it. This was the beauty of that party. Or was it a place? Everything went on naturally. Even the most unnatural things went on naturally. There was none to take note of aberrations.

New Year was a fortnight away. But fresh questions raised their heads. The downy-lipped, bosomy girl asked me, 'Don't you find answers scattered all over?' For whatever purpose it might be, these answers normally stood on the internal realities of my mind. When T. Vilayati, the moustached man, described me as 'promiscuous', I looked at Ms Pash, his short to-be-wife—her bones leaving her skin. Then I realized why he described me to be 'promiscuous'. It had taken no time for Vilayati to collect the courage to misunderstand an unusual man like me. Was Vilayati too possessive of Ms Pash?

⁂

A stupefying time. Wheels of fortune bring one to amazing times. Don't you agree? You came by bus, I, by train. You took four hours, I seven—to cover the same distance but we reached the same day, the same place. Destiny has that definition—meeting at the same time at the same place or not. The case is crystal clear—you rejoice or repent. Destiny is what it is. Then, the voice broke into my thoughts. It was the hostel manager's voice and with reverence in his eyes, he requested us, 'Please move to the lounge.' His high-pitched, hurried voice signalled something—the arrival of great soul, the revered second-in-command.

Four things counted a lot for us—the lounge, the bearers, the menu, and the ageing and swarming ladies. The lounge had three doors—two small ones and a big one, the latter being for the biggies to enter. Separation was easily identified. And there was one more door through which no one entered. Abstract objects too have destiny. Destiny—the greatest graveyard for elements that hoodwink like memory, which ditch you at the most appropriate time, in the most appropriate place.

⁂

I have travelled so far in time and distance that sometimes it feels like things haven't changed at all. I still remember, my friend: that six-and-a-half feet tall red jacket-wearing gentleman, on that sparse, uncrowded railway platform. It was 11.55 p.m. His decency and courtesy brought him to the compartment door, half-open; passengers inside were sleeping and snoring. He was to go further. I got down with my only asset in the world then—my holder which had in it a few clothes, plenty of books, a pair of almost totally worn-out slippers and half a bottle of rum to help me brave the cold. I held my friend's hand, or he mine? It was a firm handshake. 'It is the end. Don't expect any letters from me; don't hope to meet me again. Too much. It has been too much.' I waved my hands to say adieu to my friend and then the train left. So did my friend. But his words stayed with me, forever.

Sadness has many dimensions and when I remember about my friend, his is the one that captures me emotionally. Every platform, to me, presents itself philosophically: there are clean portions, there are unclean ones. Sometimes they are lit up, at others they are dark—in the latter, beggars and dogs cosy together. Sleeping partners. This world offers us iniquitous scenarios. Some sleep with call girls costing ten thousand bucks a night, some with stray dogs, free of charge. Really, this world is an unequal world. I went towards that unlit part of the platform, opened my bottle of rum, then almost finishing it, I kept the bottle aside. It was half past one. I was nervous. And I was now thinking in retrospect. Now at this moment—long gaps, I am asking myself and my friend this question. Okay. I agree my friend had had a troubled childhood and he was, in fact, a by-product of a troubled relationship; he took pleasure in talking about Sartre. This was happening in 1984. My friend used to tell me, sex is sex, pleasure is pleasure, a child is a consequence. You are not wrong, my dear. I read Sartre later, his autobiography, *Words*, and find you correct my friend. 'I was lucky to belong to a dead man: a dead man had poured out the few drops of sperm which are the normal price of a child.' But, then it happens with all. Your father did what all fathers have been doing since human beings came to this planet and will be doing till eternity.

My mind takes diversions and I have to get back to the anatomy and halos now.

Cloyingly true bureaucrats share one quality: without looking at the one in front, they pronounce their judgement on the one in the front. This happened with me one day. 'There is more to you than meets the eye.' My boss means what he says, 'I don't mince words.' Yet another common refrain he shares with the whole lot. Such remarks conveyed with alacrity, confound my personality further. Not that these show me a path as psychiatrists with their grim faces and stern looks would have me believe. Somewhere down the road these remarks make me feel one with them— their content and context. Their inseparability seems to be a pious impossibility.

∫

'You need something?' the firm-voiced gentleman sitting beside me asked politely. In his demeanour, he appeared business-like, sober, no-nonsense, and not much gregarious.

'No, nothing particular. I will see you tomorrow. We will go to the classroom together,' I responded. I had an easy feeling that this man would make a good acquaintance, if not friend. He was 6 feet 5 inches tall. And it was in his context that I had thought of the height of the doorway connecting the lounge to the dining hall. As he passed through the lounge covering a distance of twenty feet, roughly, while many eyes surveyed him questioningly, he did not so much as cast a cursory look at any of them. They were about thirty fellows altogether. Not much could be known at that point of time, but what was not amiss was this—the group promised to be a basket of completely heterogeneous commodities. Already it was past nine, I was in a haste to reach the bed, totally oblivious of the unconventionality of this habit in the hostel of this prestigious institute, the lessons about the ethos of which I had learnt from the second-in-command the other day.

∫

I rushed to my room. Room number twenty-eight. Remember St Petersburg? Why the hell do I always remember Dostoevsky? Nine beds, you see. And each bed measured six by three. A very tiny stool, wooden, was placed in between two beds. So tiny I didn't understand why the nasty thing was kept there at all. The white cat mewed. Lo and behold. As if we had a dearth of space! Nine chaps and one cat. Now this was sure to disturb my sleep. Would disturb my sleep, I feared. Okay, first let me piss. I did not want to get up after three or four hours to ease myself. Winter is bad. You frequent the loo. Summers, that way, are good. Gulp down ten glasses of water a day, and urinate thrice a day.

Memories. Storage and then retrieval. Unwanted, undesirable memories and wanted, desirable memories. And then you have conscious, subconscious and unconscious parts of your mind. It's like a psychoanalyst's dream paradigm. With my hippocampus neutral, I am totally at a loss to transfer unwanted memories into my subconscious mind. With equal ease, all things, good or bad are out and then you are condemned. You are then considered unpolished, uncouth and dishonest. But I don't mind it. And nay, I have not forgotten anything or most of the things. That is my problem. My memory is a huge pain. Nothing gets erased from there. I possess a very effective retrieval system. It's all in the game. Good enough. I have few friends and foes aplenty. No well-wishers. All fuckers. You know. But no stooping please. My spine is well erect. That is how I am. Men and women dub me anything. I choose not to react.

And nay, I had not forgotten that well-dressed chap. The cat mewed, waved his tail. Slowly, and then fast. She was still not friendly. It was about that strange-voiced girl in the dining room. One is at great pains to explain the guttural sounds of strange-voice of the girl. When unable to say anything or think anything, be serious. That was the image the well-dressed gentleman carried with himself. He lived less out of curiosity and the penchant for knowledge and more out of a trend to show off, reaching bookshelves in the library, taking a book—normally thick volumes of Dante, Shakespeare, Joyce or Henry James—and then looking at these with a saintly composure, giving a feeling that nothing but books and his good self were there at that moment.

In the morning, we were five. Another joined. From South India or Bihar. Can't guess. Had I seen him in the dining room? Who was this man? Of course, not a woman. Was he the 'Look that way' chap? God knows. Only the morning would meet my quest. He must be a carefree man. How did I know? I saw his bag and baggage the other day. A big black suitcase. And an airbag. Dumped on the mattress. He had not bothered to arrange them properly. And yeah, lying near the airbag was a book, *Selected Works of T.S. Eliot*. Eliot is a poet. That much I know. Nothing beyond that. So it must be a selection of his poems. This chap must be studious. The book was a paperback edition. On the cover was the poet's face. As I was immersed in the cover, I was distracted by a sound coming from the bathroom. It was a coughing sound. And then the sound of water, flowing down the wash basin. The lights then went dim. Only for a few seconds and then they came back to normal. There was some movement in the bathroom, some sounds and then he came out. He was puffing a cigar. Smoke curls reaching out, upwards. My introduction to him was damn formal. In fact, formality was written all over his personality. He wore a neat and crisp white shirt, trousers the crease of which was dead intact, a rosy tie. Credit to the man. Must have travelled a lot before reaching room number twenty eight. The cigar was firmly in his lips. A little initial conversation started in English. And what good, impeccable English it was. These students from the southern part of India are much better in English. My uncle once told me after finishing one of the plays by Sheridan. He asked me to learn English either from John Milton or from Dr Radhakrishnan. The first was a poet, the second, a philosopher. I tried my hands at both, but could hardly match the oratory skills of these men from down south. You pay a price for your schooling in municipal-run schools. Low fees—that is how these schools are known in public. Poor education haunts you till your death. Second-in-command's sharp, critical observations about my home town came to haunt me again. His comments were focussed on schooling. Ethos of the prestigious college, culture of the organization, billiards table, suited-booted young recruits talking, behaving purposelessly, lawn tennis, hot tomato and chicken soups, French toast. Black buttoned-up coat, black trousers, well-polished shoes, mandatory tie, flying hi-hellos, continental dinner, heavy-lidded second-in-command.

It was five in the evening. Everyone had left for indulging in their evening pleasures. I decided to try it. If the moustached man could do it, why couldn't I? I entered the washroom and locked the room from inside. Standing before the mirror, I squeezed my lips trying to throw a flying kiss. In return, I felt a pressure in my tummy and then a light fart. That was the end of my experimentation with flying kisses.

Almost thirty years have vanished. I recall some of the gatherings. In fact, all gatherings have been alike. In the right corner facing the table, cookies and coffee were spread out. Eaters, over enthusiastic ones, had no respect for the queue. Not a long one. P. Chandrika, the talkative gentleman headed the queue. But did he not say that he was a frugal eater? Yes, he did. His physique lent support to such a pronouncement. Then, why hurry? I observed. Observation is not an intellectual activity. Wrote a renowned economist Professor

A.K. Sen, 'To the silent observer.' I noticed the slip given to me. It was a small piece of paper. Brownish white. Thick. Good handwriting. Moderately large. Appealing. Did not have the guts to ask who she was? But I hazarded a guess and that must be the long-faced lady: R. Jameera. That wintry night. Bonfire. 'Your reaction,' they had insisted. 'Come on. Come on. By Jove. Say something, man.'

'Silence is golden,' I had retorted.

Clapping and clapping. Again clapping.

'Good heavens.'

'We made him speak.'

'The chap opened his mouth.'

Three comments.

⁓

Sunlight had already illuminated the thickly-curtained hall in which six fellows were still in occupation of the bed; one or two were snoring, the sound was reasonably audible. I was confronted with one of the most unexpected questions from the six-and-a-half-footer. He had already shaved once and was repeating the ritual. The lotion on his hands was slightly greenish. He kept that in a small bottle which had no logo, no stickers, nothing. There was no knowing the identity of the lotion. I guess he was too possessive about the lotion as about everything else.

'What do you think of the chap? I mean, second-in-command.'

'Am I an authority on second-in-command?' One question led to another.

'You are an authority on nothing. You spent long languishing hours with him yesterday.'

'Well, okay. Not hours but about forty minutes. If you mean that, then to hell with him.'

'Unmindful of what you might think of me, I feel you will

have a gala time ahead.'

The heavy-lidded second-in-command. So surprised at my schooling, my teachers, my heroics. How did I view him? He persisted. Cryptically. Excessively curious. I, myself, thought over that issue. Was it not natural? He dubbed me a fool and before that girl with a strange voice!

I remember I was asked a question I considered very pertinent. 'Had Gehna not been present when you were humiliated, would your views have been different?'

'Maybe. Possibly yes.'

'He called you a confused chap.'

'No, never.' I stressed my memory.

'Nevertheless, how do you plan your day? Should we go for a long stroll?' Further conversation no longer seemed to interest him. He had already gone downstairs twice to ask for tea, but a holiday for young recruits was a holiday for mess employees too. They worked on holidays when some VIPs were to visit the prestigious institute.

'No plans as yet. You decide. I will abide.'

'Obedient.'

'Yes, friendship means that.'

'Then why don't you go and get me some tea.'

'No need, sir. I have come,' entering the hall, Hay-Ram spoke a bit loudly. He was carrying a flask and two empty cups. Young recruits were expected not to insist for plates.

'Hay-Ram ji, is there any story behind not giving plates to us?' We, from the cow belt, were used to pouring tea on plates and then sipping it once it was cool. Hay-Ram, being in a holiday mood, did smile out of a sense of generosity but did not reply.

The clock struck ten. One of the seven had gotten up and was glancing through the local newspaper—one day old.

'Rape of a hen. Night at ten. What a piece of news!'

'A wise man indeed. Can he now be tried for criminal offence?'

'If not there, then at least under prevention of cruelty against animals. Don't you think raping a hapless hen is indeed cruel?'

'Hmm,' he muttered as Hay-Ram picked up a young recruit's shoes for polishing.

'It should shine properly. The first-in-command is coming for dinner tomorrow.'

'I know, saar. I have seen many such parties hosted for the first-in-command.' Hay-Ram's indifference was difficult to miss.

⁓

So, green fried peas it was. After much haggling with the local vendor, in fact a boy of thirteen or fourteen years, the price was settled. Two packets for 75 paise. Another vendor asked us to have a coconut. 'Have coconut sir. Two rupees per piece. Full of fibre. Lot of roughage.' These bloody cold places have one more drawback—they give you constipation. And constipation leads to piles. Oh, for three days in a row I still remember. It was sickening to have no bowel movement for these many days. Piles—that agonizing ailment! There was no option but to go to the doctor who gently enquired, 'Is it in your family?' I couldn't recall as such but did remember that father used to spend a hell lot of time in the toilet, much to the misery of others. So picture this. There was one toilet, desi-style and twenty applicants. My father's employers once threatened him for coming late. No problem. He changed his timings. No wee hours now and it came as a sigh of relief for nineteen members of the family. The doctor was now investigating me further. 'And you have BP also. 140/90. At your age. What did you tell me? Twenty-three-and-a-half. And your weight—fifty-three. Height—5 feet 11 inches. Boy, you are too thin and undernourished. Are you tense? Did someone die in your family of heart failure? Of brain haemorrhage?' The doctor's questions were coming to me in full pace and I was trying to rely heavily on my memory. My grandfather slept comfortably in the night but was found dead in the early morning. God was very merciful to him. He suffered no pain. But I can't remember, maybe it was kidney failure. I was now thinking harder. Was there a case of lunacy in my family? Yes, there was this Pagla Chacha (mad uncle). Lacked vision. He used to talk loudly not making any sense. The doctor was listening attentively and with concern now. 'Is there a case of alcoholism in the family?' I recall that someone did die in an accident in the family and when the postmortem was done, it was discovered that it was a case of alcoholism! The concerned doctor now gave his final verdict—'Complete check-up recommended. Fix an appointment through my compounder. Any time. After a fortnight. Your BP worries me. Piles at this age is worrisome.'

My six-and-a-half-footer friend was watching meticulously. Listening attentively, sympathetically and smiling.

I was, as expected, a backbencher. It was noticed by none other than that heee-heee girl. All was pre-planned. This theory got full-fledged support outside. Bosh-Bosh, the main propagator of the theory of planning. Planning is the panacea for all ills, I cited. Suspicion: the main anchor of the ethos. No, sir, you are too good. It's so good for you to invite us. We must play host to you first. Madam is also invited. 'Yeah, yeah,' shouted the three from the group. 'We must. We must,' that plump man, who had labelled me promiscuous, was most vocal. But the short lady was mum. The giggling lady was on the job. As said, it was all pre-planned. And interestingly, second-in-command was privy to it. So, it seemed. 'Your cooking skills are well known, here and far afield. Let us then do like this,' the plump fellow suggested, 'We request sir to bless us with the output of his cookery skills. And we will bear expenses. A good dinner on Saturday evening. Sunday being a holiday there will be no hurry in the morning. No rushing to classes. Do you all agree?' Yes, yes. The rest of the group was left with no option. Some murmuring here and there but it was unnoticeable. The lanky man laughed submissively. Much to my chagrin, the man was notoriously silent. The short lady advised the plump fiancée to look into the affairs personally. She had a message to be conveyed. 'I wouldn't be joining,' declared six-and-a-half-footer. You have some engagements, I suppose. No. But I hate such gatherings. Why the hell the second-in-command should cook if we have to bear the expenses? No way. The lanky chap again laughed. This time, stupidly. His laughter was a substitute for his forced silence.

There was this beggar whom I had seen several times. I saw him at the same place but at different times. He wore the same blanket, brown and torn, here and there. His entire persona was very mysterious. He was totally covered save for that one finger. There were coins near him. One can easily guess that his earnings were anywhere near three to four thousand rupees per month. At that time it was more than double of our salary. One day, I could not help. Why not observe him for a sufficiently long time? Mere observation is not an intellectual activity. Is observing a beggar an intellectual activity? Let me know. Why is he totally covered? I spent an hour observing the beggar. It was a lazy Sunday. My friends were keen to know what I found in that beggar. But I, as usual, was on my own trajectory. 'Don't compound the narration. Defer for some other time. You have a derisive habit. You bring in all sorts of things when you narrate. Tell me why the beggar was covered or covered himself. You watched him for an hour. Good investigation. Man. Well. KK, that day you mentioned about something. Investigative scrutiny...' my six-and-a-half-footer friend asked me. I told him, 'My father told me that a good auditor is one who knows arithmetic. Simple one. Plain one. But not algebra. Algebra was my bête noire.

The bloody discipline had humbled me so many times. Algebra was no worse than vital statistics. Always changing. No perfect measurements. Vital statistics elude perfect measurement. That is what statistics is all about. My father believed in plain arithmetic. And was sacked. He turned out to be a bad auditor.'

Ms Pash, the short lady, was in great haste to reveal to everyone her deep love for her 'catch'. The portly, moustached man was prince charming for her; everything about him was remarkable—his style of talking, mouthing unheard, unfamiliar words, unusually attractive gestures, his flying kisses that could be felt in air only, his exquisiteness, the big, luxurious car he drove in posh locations in Delhi, and above all his love for his newly acquired asset—Ms Pash, the short lady.

Years later. It's in R.B. Sheridan's *The Rivals*. And in it, it is the same moustached man who reads—

> 'Faulk. She's gone! For ever. There was an awful resolution in her manner, that riveted me to my place. O fool! Dolt! Barbarian! Curst as I am, with more imperfections than my fellow-wretches... O love! Tormentor! Fiend! whose influence, like the moon's, acting on men of dull souls, makes idiots of them, but meeting subtler spirits, betrays their course, and urges sensibility to madness.'

A sound was heard. It was of the arrival of a car. It was an old fiat, grey and newly painted. Windows had plain glasses, not the tainted ones. Headlights had their upper portions painted black which was done to mitigate accidents. There was a bottle on the back seat visible from the outside. It was a bottle of whiskey,

1000 ml. Johnny Walker, Red Label. Imported scotch, whiskey—these were definitely indicative of status. Steeply priced at around eight hundred rupees those days, it was not an easily affordable drink. It added lustre to parties. Two drinks and all obscurities would be smoothened. And most importantly, it does not give you a hangover like the local brands. However, the bottle inside appeared empty. There were just traces of some liquid moving inside the bottle. It was colourless, plain, distilled liquid. Can you imagine a liquor bottle not containing liquor? Removing the key, the gentleman turned around on his seat. Pushing himself slightly up, he lifted the bottle and drank the plain liquid. Water. The gentleman then stepped out of the car. The front door was half open and first came out his right leg. He was wearing black shoes. Not a new pair but they were polished. His socks were white and his blue trousers properly ironed. An orderly hastened to open the door. And the gentleman now fully alighted from the car.

'How are you, Khilari?' inquired the gentleman addressing the orderly, a man of sixty and not from Bihar.

'Pine (fine), chir (sir). Madam has not come,' the orderly had problems with pronouncing a few letters.

'She has other engagements.'

'People will mich (miss) her, chir (sir).' Further probing did not enamour the gentleman. Three young boys of twenty-two to twenty-eight were deputed to receive the gentleman and though they moved forward to receive him, they received scant attention as the gentleman did not consider them worthy of any notice.

'Can I get you the bottle, chir, very cold, chir?' Khilari seemed talkative.

'The bottle does not have what you think, Khilari. I have stopped drinking for some time now.' Khilari looked suspicious. He knew these brown sahibs too well, having interacted with them for long and also having seen them interacting among themselves.

The latter was more relevant.

'Johnny Walker is a costly brand, chir. Difficult to even chee (see) these things here nowadays.'

'I know. But the one inside my car has warm water. I take warm water.'

'Warm water in costly bottle,' Khilari sighed.

Someone sneezed. And it was second-in-command who repeated it.

'Should I call for a doctor? One resides in the adjacent house. He will be happy to come here and treat you. At least you will get immediate relief. Party should be enjoyed, sir,' one of the three gentleman 'Ps', failing to resist his temptation further to influence the second-in-command, inquired very politely, his voice conveying concern about the second-in-command's health. The other two 'Ps' nodded positively but suspected the designs of the first 'P'.

'Khilari, go immediately and fetch the doctor. Sir can take rest in the lounge. Let the doctor see him and then we can escort him to the lawn.' The second 'P' issued directions to the orderly who could not hide his unwillingness to make any move. Khilari was well acquainted with the hierarchical positions and considered it infra dig to obtain directions from the ones other than/those at the top. He looked at the second-in-command's face to see his reaction, which did not favour with approval to the concerns of the three 'Ps'.

'It is all right, Khilari, I am okay. But, anyway, let the doctor, what did you say his name was, come. Let us wait in the lounge,' the second-in-command said and moved towards a door that was to lead him to the lounge. But what was really remarkable was his sense of detachment from the three gentleman 'Ps'. He did not bother to even acknowledge the good gestures from the any of the 'Ps'. And while seating him on a cushioned sofa, he closed his eyes, only partially, and through those half-closed eyes surveyed the boys without letting them realize about his intentions. The survey was on and so was his thought process. What was he thinking about? The three 'Ps'. Poor boys. Juniors. Rather very junior. Inexperienced, immature and new kids who were placed very low in the hierarchy. And yes, they were not to be trusted easily. They are the ones through whom gossip travels wide and fast. They are considered highly talkative and totally unimaginative. They are jovial but misguided chaps who don't look as if they are serious in life and don't know how to talk to seniors. The optimist always looked at the brighter side of life. So do these youngsters. Fame. Money. Fiancés. Rich. Not necessarily beautiful. But necessarily dominating with no less dominating mothers-in-law.

∫

The unperturbed and vibrant mind is an outcome of the diametrically opposite positions the bureaucrat has held in his more than thirty years of service. The three gentleman 'Ps' still in wait outside, hoping to be noticed. Three gentleman 'Ps' already on the job training, learning basic lessons on bureaucratic meanderings.

Coming back to the present, as I prepare to move forward, let me assure the readers—whether others come or not, Professor Yadav and the six-and-a-half-footer friend are going to be my constant company throughout, the latter, many times unconsciously.

CHAPTER 7

The Psychiatrist and Awareness

It was a quiet night, a quiet sleep, a quiet dream. I saw an old woman in white coming near me. She kissed my lips. Her age had dwarfed the warmth of her kiss but I could feel it. The strangest thing about her was her face. She had no face, only lips. Outside the windows, hefty clouds were driving the shy moon away to an unknown place. Her lips sill lingered on mine. Her lips were, however, lifeless. She didn't have any teeth in fact. She kissed me twice and then many times. I stood disenchanted like a man on the verge of entering a zone of ambiguity.

∽

I wish that old lady could convert into a pretty, young girl. I engaged Professor Yadav over the logic of this dream. He assumed a lot of air; breathed meaningfully. Thoughtful as he was, he raised his eyebrows as high as he could before he opened his mouth, 'KK, anybody can look at a pretty girl and see a pretty girl. An artist can look at a pretty girl and see the old woman she will become. A better artist can look at an old woman and see the pretty girl that she used to be.'

'Better artist means... I am no artist?' my query seemed

harmless at least to me.

'Yeah, you are not, I know. A great artist—a master, who should I name? Okay,' he seemed going wayward; his forehead stressed, he was in search of a name. Names do matter in fields like art and culture. 'Okay, what of Auguste Rodin. Heard his name?' His eyes threw questions suspecting if I knew it. I shook my head; he seemed pleased. 'He was a great artist. He could look at an old woman, portray her exactly as she was…and force the viewer to see the pretty girl she used to be… More than that, he can make anyone with the sensitivity of an armadillo. You know KK, age dulls us but beauty lives through us imprisoned inside our ruined body.' I was stunned hearing him. 'KK, after all, it is an endless tragedy that there was never, not a girl born who ever grew older without being eighteen in her heart…no matter what the merciless hours have done to her. But what of us dear? Growing old doesn't matter to both of us: you and me; we never desire admiration but there are different people. And yes, coming to your dream, you must see a psychiatrist urgently.'

∽

Isn't it astonishing how a psychiatrist picks up on people's moods from what they write or speak? This man I am going to meet is a psychiatrist—a therapist; he is the one who tells people to buy Anthony de Mello's book, *Awareness*. de Mello was a priest and therapist/poet who wrote this book to help people overcome life's issues; the book is spiritual in nature and truly a great book to look at one's self. The worrying part is that it states we are all born sleeping, marry sleeping, etc. It says that we need to wake up, find our true meaning, wake ourselves up to the beauty and loveliness of human existence, no matter what our religion/theology is. We are unanimous about one thing: all that is well, is well. Professor Yadav's words flashed in my mind: 'The psychiatrist is harsh, but effective. Trust him and get well soon. You are mentally ill, KK. Bear it in mind.'

It was 10.30 in the morning and I was in front of the psychiatrist's chamber. It was a large imposing room containing two chairs and a big table. One chair was for the psychiatrist and the other for his client. His voice was austere, like that of a galling bird. Without looking at me, he asked me to talk about my problems. Where his eyes fell, was unclear. His eyeballs were fixated, but where—that was a mystery to me. He warded off my doubts, 'Please go ahead. I am listening. Talk normally. Don't be conscious of yourself. Just speak of your issues.'

'I occasionally have dreams, terrible ones. These wake me up with nauseating feelings. It has been happening to me frequently. For the past one week, I have had dreams that make the reality around me distorted. I am left in a virtual state. What should I say? How should I describe that?'

'Problem in recollection. Wretched dreams entail that. Now time to put some stress on your memory. Not much, but a little.' While his glance was still somewhere else, the tone and tenor in which he uttered his words were the same—stony, unconcerned, detached.

'Something like a subject in any such wretched dream. My acquaintances think of me as living in a state of diffused restlessness. I have feelings of inadequacy, a disturbed gait and nervous movements. I imagine situations that are catastrophic in nature. These stem from real-life situations, but they are terrifying and incongruous, not at all relevant to real-life situations.'

For the first time, the psychiatrist looked at me—for thirty seconds—trying as if to figure out something, but his poker face denied me any access to what he was thinking.

'Do you have fixed patterns? How do all these dreams end? What do they culminate into?' His questions came to me as if out of a mummy's mouth. His struggle with words was remarkable.

'Culminate into? Okay. It goes nowhere—that is the issue. It ends around three in the morning or five, I am not very certain. But when I am awake, I think of what awoke me. What wakes me up from a highly disturbing sleep is a medley of wrinkled images, hypnagogic ones.'

'That's what I need. What awakens you? I need to know it,' said the psychiatrist.

The day with him ended there.

My second session with the psychiatrist was about to begin. I continued, 'This has happened to me now on three to four mornings. I wake up almost unable to breathe and start to sweat profusely. My pillow covers become wet due to the sweating. I have to rush to the bathroom to clear out what apparently feels like being stuck in my throat but nothing comes out. There is a nauseating feeling inside me but after some time the restlessness goes away and I calm down starting to breathe normally. This entire process takes two to three hours. But by the time everything settles, the dawn is breaking. Since it is becoming a routine, I never feel fresh in the morning and my anxiety has been on the rise.'

'Have you ever tried to locate the cause?' the psychiatrist was tepid as usual. 'Every time I feel like evaluating the circumstances, I find a chain of apprehensions—demoralizing and depressing. The harder I try to find out why the anxieties suffocate me, I get no answers. But, sometimes, I get some solace that one of my friends happens to be more of a neurotic than what I think of him.'

'Now this interests me. Please pause for a while.' The psychiatrist seemed genuinely keen as I noticed movement in his posture for the first time. His eyes also showed some movement. I felt enthused. 'Tell me more about your friend. Oftentimes we know of one through his or her views about their friends and acquaintances. This is a new opening for me.' The psychiatrist seemed excited now. I told him in detail about my six-and-a-half-footer friend, his red jacket, his penchant for milk, his father's troubled love for his mother, his tiny face and his sternness.

Another session came to an end.

⌒

Time: 10.30 a.m. Another day and it is my last session with him. This psychiatrist believed in only one form. His inquisitiveness was sharp as was his slothfulness. I was trying to be as honest as possible knowing the last session would end my turmoil.

'In my dreams, I did witness something I would describe as unbelievable—unbelievable in the sense that the object of the dream had been what I had never aspired for. I have trained myself in misogynous art. That is out of my aloofness and sheer compunction that comes with it. I completely withdraw from the parties in which women, irrespective of their age, built, complexion or attire, assemble. I do like and relish sex in reality as well as in fantasy but the presence of fabulously dressed women does give me a pang, the nature of which, I fail to comprehend. It is incomprehensible for me. It is a sort of hatred developed unconsciously but firmly.'

My counterpart facing me seated on the opposite chair was avidly engrossed, I suppose, in what was coming out of me. Oh, yes. This time it was a notebook in which he was jotting something down with a frown.

'I saw a complete shallowness where everything was loose, just existing, hanging here and there with no base. The dream was firm giving me a feeling of a secured place. In the vacuum, the emptiness of which was as harrowing as it was grave, was placed one chair. It appeared to be made of wood but those that resembled fresh white bones with no stains of blood. A chair is not a thing to be remembered after a dream is over but its very look was so despising, depressive and penetrating as to compel a mention of it.' I halted as I was growing tense.

'There was something more depressing for me. I saw a visage—a very familiar visage at that—and after I had seen it on the chair, I was totally at a loss to recollect it. I recollect it as the visage of a woman, a woman whose gloom was writ large within the whole of the vacuum.'

'Be clearer. I am getting an insight into your problems. But, be specific please,' the psychiatrist's words made inroads into my ears. I pressed my memory deeper.

'I realize that the woman must be thirty-five to thirty-six in age sitting very calmly, virtually motionless on that wretched chair. Her oracular silence gives her sorrow an all the more pinpricking and palpable look. Was she desirous to say a few words to someone who could feel one with her or was she intending to convey nothing but expecting someone to understand the feelings behind her look?'

'Interesting. So you have questions in your dream—lovely.' The man of wisdom seemed slightly gleeful.

'Nothing else was as vivid. These questions compounded my feelings of pathos. My inability to recall the woman's face was by no means belittling my confusion. In the meanwhile, the doorbell rang and the dream was interrupted.'

'Can you retrieve anything more?'

'No, nothing.'

'Okay. Come on the 11th at 10.30.'

'Morning or night?'

'Morning.'

Suddenly, the whole chamber was brightened and a lady, with

a big black mole on the right side of her small chin, entered the chamber signalling me to leave.

10.30, morning.

'You need awareness. Take these pills as prescribed. Nurse will brief you outside. And read Anthony de Mello's book: *Awareness*. Yeah, one more thing. Incidentally, do you masturbate too much?'

Contrary to what I was told, the psychiatrist was a cool man, not harsh at all. His lopsided smile lingers with me.

Professor Yadav was not interested in the way the psychiatrist began my treatment but he was trying to draw an inference about the psychiatrist's relationship with me. 'It's all about trust, KK. History has taught us a lesson. Trust is a great but intriguing word. It is capable of destroying many myths about those enjoying the freedom of gauging trust guised as distrust in a society. Trust entails fear of detection. Is fear of detection not embedded into the idea of trust itself? Did not Glaucon and Socrates endlessly debate if trust depended on fear of detection? So, your psychiatrist will be under a continuous strain fearing his lack of trust might be detected some day.'

'Then sir?'

'Nothing; just my views on these psychiatrists.'

'But then why did you refer me to him if you have such views on trusting psychiatrists?' I had to ask him.

'This is the beauty of mental disorders and their treatment. Follow doctor's advice carefully,' Professor Yadav counselled.

CHAPTER 8

Within the Cave or the Cave Within

Am I swayed by the idea that Michael McClure's prescient lines, which I have cited in the beginning, gives me? We meet huge figures every day, on the roads, in markets, in towers we reside, in lifts, all of us. Then huge figures meet amongst themselves. They talk to each other; they laugh and sometimes ponder; they talk about others; they rub themselves against each other; they toy with their 'self', they jettison others' selves—we all have been face to face with them. But, what about the idea of 'caves'. The word by its very nature is restrictive: it restricts relationships, communication with others, voices, expressions, possibilities, but most importantly it blurs natural growth of a large number of individuals. We have heard stories from our grandparents and parents—stories of monsters, devils, lions and hyenas living in caves. They further enlightened, 'Our forefathers lived in caves.' Does it convey compliments to our forefathers or do we look down upon our ancestors? One morning you hear a knock at your door. You open the door to be welcome by a hoary, unrecognizable man—unclad and unfed. He introduces himself as your ancestor. Will you permit him to enter your drawing room? I am sure you wouldn't unless you suffer lunacy. Caves, thus, create fear and restrict entry. Alternatively said, caves represent murkiness of edges and depths. You fear the ones who live in caves.

Kafka's diaries give ample instances of individuals in caves. One such runs like this:

It was 21 February 1911. Oscar M emerges for the first time in Kafka's diaries. Constrained, superimposed relations that he enjoyed with his father fascinate anyone interested in child/adult psychology. To a few of my friends, I explain the crux of my understanding of Oscar M's travails in these words—'Silence, silence…no ifs and no buts…only silence, silence only. Silence made his father's voice noisier. Relationship between the dead and unknown, a relationship between silence and greater silence.' Incidentally, I did not skip how lacking in sense was Dr Steiner's advice—'Eat no eggs.' One of the friends responded, 'Eat eggs but with salt.'

The summary of the above is the epitome of the cave or the caves. There are dark eyes and darker glasses; a blind man passes, followed by another blind man. Many blind men pass. Many dark eyes will cross. Many darker glasses will meet. Vision will be born on which caves will survive.

Though from a small town and educated in a nondescript university, I preferred the company of books to individuals and late night parties. High modernists identifying themselves as elitists of the society hold no attraction for me; rather, they invoke in me a sense of indifference. I have chosen to explore common themes of human condition, particularly of plebeians, a class I belong to too. Though at a price. I heard an acquaintance enquiring about me from another, 'Is he a psycho?' Elitists undertake the excruciating trouble to search for answers to such questions about men and women like me and the caves resonate with their efforts to search answers. I believe in the power of words: I write poems, books of poetry.

I find my book has become my greatest enemy. It brings me, a nondescript man, to the forefront; all eyebrows over swollen eyes get raised. I seek shelter to seek an escape route. I heard a hoarse voice enquiring, 'Who is this fellow? I have never seen him. How is his conduct?' He shouts at me but I remain unsurprised. Those in the higher echelons inherit this trait—they shout at those in lower and those farther beneath those in a lower position—that is how we move from one generation to another; that is how we evolve and civilize ourselves. Our brethren boast of their inheritance, one which is full of loss. Amazingly, even others think loss creates enemy, foes, malice and woes. The one who is shouting at me I should pity. Enslaved by his own peers for that long, is he not a burden passed onto us by those genetically and hierarchically superior to him? A dull dying entity on the verge of his own moral extinction? Everything, in the modern caves, is predetermined—nothing moves without a nod. I cannot think of better ways to look at them: they are factotums—incapacitated to think, to talk, to smile and above all to behave. 'I hope you are understanding what I mean when I speak of modern caves?' My six-and-a-half-footer red jacket-wearing friend is sipping milk sitting beside me on a stool. He nods in agreement. So appeasing.

January 2006, Gurgaon: Madam Mahavipida Devi's residence: Block F, 22nd floor, House number 2201—her spacious drawing room.

'She is a bulk, a knot/swollen in space.' Atwood's landlady is a common feature in any hierarchy.

Only a few weeks back, I visited madam's residence.

Madam is on the chair in the imposing drawing room. She was occupying the chair she had been eying for long. And then she talked about that book. 'A book in Hindi'. She kind of condescended. 'No, in English.' Keeping her eyes peeled—'Your wife has written it? Does she know English? Is she from Delhi?'

'No, I have.'

Her eyes became wider and wider. 'You have written?' There was utter disbelief in her. 'Okay. Fine.'

While my conversation with her had quite a few negations, in the modern hierarchical system, a normal conversation would have so many 'yeses' peppered by 'madams' and 'sirs'.

'Yes, madam, yes, madam.'

'How come you are stationed at such a place? How long has it been? Completed two years.'

'Yes, madam.'

'Move from there immediately.'

'Where?'

'Oh, oh, you don't meet the parameters. You must understand that. '

'Yes, madam. Parameters. Which parameters madam? None told me of them.'

'Yes, you don't meet these. Do I owe you an explanation? I know you fellows from the cow belt.'

'Yes, madam. But what is my fault? Me, why only me. There are so many. Why only me?'

'Shut up. And leave my house immediately.'

'Yes madam.'

And then there is darkness. Light never appears. Someone falls somewhere in the cave. But the cave is silent like Oscar M. or noisy like his father. I left madam's house, shocked and disgusted. I take the lift from the 22nd floor to the ground floor. Press push button 0: ground floor. No one is with me. It's a high-speed lift. 19th disappears; 18th emerging. The electricity goes off, the lift halts. Emergency light flickers. No one is with me and auditory hallucinations are creeping into my ears; voices coming from within my brain. Two women talk:

'I was hunting for you, yesterday. Where were you all day?'

'Busy, you knowhn (know). Shifting luggage to new house in Tilak Lane, you knowhn.'

'Did you get an offer for first change only now? You are running ninth year here.'

'No got thrice but did not accept, you knowhn.'

'Why?'

'Previously smaller-sized flats. But this time, you knowhn. Four big bed rooms, four big bathrooms, big garden in front, big backyard, two servant quarters, you knowhn. This one much bigger, you knowhn. But now at least you must be ready to move. Twelve years you have spent here. You knowhn.'

'Don't worry... I will...'

Electricity comes, voices cease. Ground floor. Doors open. I step out. Voices have ceased completely. I wish I could have heard the other lady's complete response.

Why should I mention it? Of what interest can it be to any one? It's a perfect example of what happens when ordinariness, which makes a man in the street like me, is confronted with extraordinariness of a few people who make the 'elite of upwardly moving society.'

The lady was a prisoner of her own captivity. I pity this woman who, fortified by an elevated sense of her position swallowed her sanity to reach an intersection she preferred to sit on, unable to occupy it or leave it, making it impossible for anyone to try anything else. She should have heard the song Cleopatra. She was so good in shouting and banging the receiver of the telephone.

My soliloquy is on where I come across my six-and-a-half-footer friend giving me a hard look and enquiring whether I met Joe P.K. for whom he had as much respect as I had. 'Joe loves to tell stories. Did you meet him? When, where?' I was amazed to hear my friend's voice. He speaks so rarely. But I assured him I would meet Joe shortly. I knew, like my friend, Joe too was rebellious by nature. I kept my promise.

March 2013. A small village in Madhya Pradesh.

Joe P.K. Pardon my honesty, but I have to tell you. Some people are nasty human beings. Take for instance Khandu (father-in-law) versus Shukar-Nar (his son-in-law). Of both the father-in-law and the son-in-law, Conrad was so apt when he wrote: 'He was obeyed, yet he inspired neither love nor fear, nor even respect. He inspired uneasiness. That was it. Uneasiness.'

'Incidentally, have you seen Khandu, his daughter and his son-in-law? Can you tell me what is common in them?' Joe quipped.

'No.'

'Okay. They are alike. You can't distinguish between a man and a woman. You cannot make out if you are looking at their faces—who is Khandu, who is his daughter and who is his son-in-law, Shukar-Nar. Their faces are alike. I saw them many times together. So that was it.'

His goodness offended many. Joe is now 95, while in his heyday, he spared none and rightly so. It was so typical of him. I was keen to meet him though he offered to drop in sometime at my convenience. I hesitated and he agreed to my going to his residence. I was with him at the anointed time. 'Some coffee?' a voice came from inside and I sighted a youngish looking boy moving behind the curtains and expecting a reply from Joe who chose not to respond and let the boy decide on his own—the best way to tackle uncertainties.

'Farewell speeches serve an intended purpose when it comes to delivering your worst accumulated dreams to your peers and juniors.' I thought of sharing what recently Shukar-Nar on his superannuation, unashamedly and unrestrainedly talked of; slapping the collective face of what he once was a miniscule portion of, but as I said worst dreams are best delivered in worst forms, on the day an unwilling gathering is all set to say, 'Good riddance, bugger.' Joe was dense in his absorptions; eyes half-closed, in an obvious struggle with his old age. He seemed to raise his hands to suggest something. His body movements were slow and he was struggling because of his old age. His memory was also waxing and waning. 'Is he not Khandu's son-in-law?' Not waiting for my reply (I did not know who this Khandu was), he found the answer on his own, 'He is.' A long pause ensued, Joe groping into his memory. Unexpectedly, he laughed or at least I sensed he laughed and felt tempted to enquire why he laughed. 'Like father-in-law, like son-in-law. Made for each other—you know.' He laughed cheerfully; clearly, meaningfully, vividly conveying he connected correctly. And then, the coffee arrived.

Joe was not easy to fall victim to irksomeness: a constant cough—a peculiar noise heard each time phlegm encroached upon his lungs or throat or both (he ended the innings by softly saying—Oh, shit…) did not bemuse him but he was serene. He wanted the story to be finished early. He lived his breaths hesitatingly, perhaps he knew what awaited him for long. I liked his truthfulness: he did not seem to be bamboozling himself. For him, the end lay in realities well-told. Its absence suffocated him; he waited for his breath to come smoothly. 'Then dear, shit, where I was?' He wondered as if there was no one except him. 'Khandu was a very short fellow, you know, hardly reaching five feet or is it an exaggeration? Okay, let me say four-and-a-half.' Joe believed in precision; he consciously portrayed his belief in precise details. He was weighing his utterances carefully and above all, though sometimes he would look at me, his whole conversation seemed to be a monologue. 'Khandu was a rogue, harsh fellow bemusing himself with his gigantic personality as he believed it to be. Great men often have great many delusions. And those delusions shatter on the day such men superannuate. Am I sounding ovine? Are you bored? If you do not like this conversation we can switch over to some other things.'

'No, no it interests me,' I mumbled.

'Good. Some more coffee?' Without waiting for my reply, he pushed the bell twice, and the same youngish boy shouted, 'Okay. I will get it to you in five minutes.' It was all mechanical relationships.

⸻

Joe's next observations took me by utter surprise. 'You think rebellion is a good thing. Nay let me raise a more basic one—is it a good word? Do you think all of us must rebel, at least once… once at least in our lifetime? Men may come and men may go; women may come and women may go. I want someone to tell me—let rebels stay for good. Let this tribe of people stay.' Joe took almost ten minutes to say these words; weighing each word he muttered as if a wrong word would result in grave injustice. Then he coughed or perhaps laughed—the sound was inaudibly low. 'Remember dear, nothing will change, nothing. You told me of Khandu's son-in-law. Okay, let me take for example, the world of bureaucracy. There you have permanent sons-in-law and daughters-in-law. You know coterie. Five-six fellows from both gender form a coterie to control higher-ups in the hierarchy. Wrong dear. Pardon me. Everyone is a law unto himself and herself and the greatest lawmaker (God) sleeps soundly in his large chamber on a chair that magnifies his frame.' God? The childish-looking boy entered bringing two mugs of coffee and four medium-sized biscuits and while he placed these on the teapoy which was nearer to Joe than me, he asked me if I could help myself with coffee and biscuits. Before I answered him, he took the mug and handed it over to me. He was a boy of sixteen or so, fragile with a slight beard on his otherwise charming face. He never looked into my eyes and all through his presence, Joe remained calm; his restlessness calmed by the boy's presence. I ate one biscuit, a local flavour, but there was no taste. Joe insisted that I have one more but I declined. He seemed to be trying to come back to the present. 'You say you are frustrated. I could not agree more. Imagine my plight: the man I used to have my drinks with, to have non-veg jokes with, once at the top of the hierarchy in the cave refused to recognize me. He took six days to give me an appointment and that too was to materialize two weeks later. Bastards have the same colour, you know; they fart out the same wind. That was when I realized I must rebel—the two equals had suddenly become unequals. I ought to have gauged the man's supposed invincibility. But, for that I needed a platform and there was none. I had no grounds, no support, none to push me inside. Or outside of my fears. I wish I could have killed my fears then. I would have emerged a rebel. I had wealth, a wife who was still alive and my sons were well-settled but still I lacked that which propelled the rebellion inside a man. Now, in retrospect, sometimes, I feel I could have killed that man with my fist; just broken his head as one breaks a small watermelon and then gone and surrendered to the local police station saving the police inspector all the toil not worth investigating this man's murder.' Joe stopped to sip his coffee and having done that sighed, 'Oh shit...' I wanted to ask him why the intermittent 'Oh shit...' but fearing he might lose rhythm, I decided to let it pass. The young boy was peeping inside.

∫

'You are a Hindu. You believe in the revival of Hinduism but you are not even opening your mouth. Say something about rebellion. See how Hinduism is spreading fast. Now let me tell you something. That great writer you know Nirad Chaudhuri. What a fantastic giant he was writing untiringly of what he thought of as Hindu acedia. Please don't mistake me. I am only recalling this gentleman who incidentally was a Hindu himself. He rebelled in whatever he wrote.'

'No he was a Hindu ignoramous.' I had to let my views be known to Joe.

'Listen. Have respect for my age.' Joe was stern.

'Nirad was as much proud of his wisdom and learning as he was ashamed of his peers lacking in these. He knew he was living in India—a land full of surprises, surmises and suspecting Hindus. So, he chose to name four gentlemen, all foreigners, whom he honoured by calling them truly learned. You tell me if you have heard these four names. Or even one.'

Before Joe could speak further, I think, he tried to break wind but could have no success with what apparently seemed his first attempt.

'Harnack, Eduard Meyer, Mommsen—these three and the fourth one—a difficult name. Yeah, it was Wilamowitz-Moellendorf. What do you think of them? Was Chaudhuri trying to take his peers for a ride or was he serious?'

'I have not heard any of these names. Please tell me something about them,' I succumbed.

'I tried to learn of these gentlemen KK. I read *The Continent of Circe* in the early eighties. Then, Wikipedia was not there. I really don't know anything about them. Where they lived, what they did, nothing. With Wikipedia now you can know of any Tom, Dick and Harry around you.'

'Sir, you mean to suggest Chaudhuri might not have named these four unknown gentlemen had Wikipedia been there then?'

'Exactly. He would have known that his lesser-learned peers would have used Wikipedian knowledge to rip Chaudhuri's knowledge apart.'

'Then sir, did you not ask anyone else about them?'

'I asked a few senior bureaucrats and some professors of universities. The bureaucrats straightway told they had not heard of Nirad Chaudhuri, not to speak of *The Continent of Circe*. Three professors had heard of him but not of his book; all of them assured they would read the book and get back. Unfortunately, none returned back.'

'Thank you, sir. Can I leave now?'

'Just give me fifteen minutes. I forget what was there in the beginning. Oh shit. Yeah. Hinduism and rebellion. I remember Chaudhuri was fond of citing from sculptures and what fascinating citations these were. Look at this.' He paused. And after a few seconds resumed the conversation. 'You know the great sage, Preceptor of the Gods, Vrihaspati. Mamata, his brother Utathya's wife, was known for her beauty. Vrihaspati desired her despite the knowledge that she was his brother's wife. Once, in Utathya's absence, Vrihaspati came by Mamata insistent on consummating his desire of Mamata. However, being pregnant, Mamata pleaded with him arguing that two children could not remain within her womb. Vrihaspati was adamant. Even the pleas of the baby inside Mamata's womb were lost on him. He, however, failed to succeed in his endeavour eventually since the baby, with his tiny feet thwarted his energy to embrace Mamata. This led to Vrihaspati cursing the baby while in the womb and Dirghatama was born blind,' Joe concluded.

'So what, sir?'

'That is rebellion. Even a small, unborn child can be rebellious when confronted with irrationality but you fellows die so many times every hour in caves. You people lack reaction, are tawdry, passive, inarticulate, uncultivated, puny.'

∫

'Have you read history? Perhaps you want to know why I refrain from commenting on the set of people—the ones who read history.

I do it intentionally. These people don't deserve any comments. They are like the salient spectators in whose lot has come the oppressive job of reading things but not thinking over them. Loathe them. Pity them. Do it by all means. But don't expect them to react. Do you know the sort of people who can react? This question you will face only in the case of human beings. Take animals. Even ants react. They bite before they die. Maybe the earthworm can be an honourable exception? I have not come across anyone with a genuine complaint that he or she has been hurt by an earthworm. It has not learnt the specialized skills in the art of reaction. So have you, the people in the cave. You cease to think, you cease to be meaningful. You might also remember their complaint. Those incapable of thinking have illuminated lives. Think of lunatics—the most fortunate ones, for they don't realize the complexities of life as they are incapacitated to think. They are without any desire to oppose.'

'If someone does not react, what could be better? Let exploitation go on, unabated. Meekly exploited creatures. Voiceless. Insipid. Turbulent bodies. Raped souls. All these have added that lustre to the sheen of modern behaviour which makes it developed as we, with full pride, call it. You fellows belong to a developed, matured cave. Don't we wallow in senseless pride? High heads, stiff neck and straight nose. Dead dance of corpses. Ones alive are worse than those dead.' Joe, having lectured for long, requested me to leave. On my way back, I wished persons like madam, Shukar-Nar and Khandu could have conducted themselves more gracefully.

⁓

Self-pity. Returning to McClure. If no one answers you, should we stop passers-by to discuss and argue with them on how to deal with caves or more importantly the ones living there? Okay. The narrations mentioned just above are instances of clever and motivated behaviour—a summed outcome of past learnings and trainings. Can caves also not be within individuals? These are unseen talents in some individuals who can rattle everyone around them. This they do it with the help of the power of remembering past things as the same McClure says, 'We are the temples of the conscious past.' They remember these at an appropriate time and place. Particularly when you meet them. Their familiarity with names and periods adds dignity to their wisdom. They know the art of defacing clean faces to hide their unclean ones. Their personages represent grotesque ornaments that they carry with them over their heads. Caves and their inhabitants have their own philosophy; they choose to go by poignancy of that. So what? There is no rational answer to 'so what?'.

CHAPTER 9

Authors, Books and Human Behaviour Chronicled

(I)

Living by books is all about faith. Books offer opportunities for an exploration into instincts that shape human actions and reactions. To discern human behaviour, it might be a good idea to be in the company of books or even better, be in the company of people who have been voracious readers of books.

∫

Professor Yadav has many habits—one of which is quoting philosophers, poets and essayists. To make one believe he is not farcical, he refers to books, chapters and pages, quoting from them, never repeating the quotations. Last night, he was at his best, giggling away while speaking to a visiting professor from Delhi University. I thought he would be able to suppress his giggles when speaking of Nassim Taleb and the latter's experiments with things unusual. 'You understand,' he was saying, 'when you know little, you become susceptible to yourself. Yeah, I think Taleb is damn right. Don't talk of books that you have read. Anyone can do that.

All these modern literary giants producing award-winning novels have been doing this—they either talk of their books or the books they have read or the books of their close friends. That way I like Taleb. As these literary giants grow older, the number of unread books on the shelves in their libraries stare at them menacingly. How I interpret Taleb is: let men and women be known by the books they have not read.'

∽

(II)

Turning towards me, Professor Yadav averred, 'KK, think over what Taleb signals. How people talk, how they behave—everything you can cover with Taleb's arguments. You look at the people around you, particularly members of the groups and coterie, and they are everywhere, and try to judge them not in terms of what they say in public but in terms of what they don't say. What they don't say, please believe me, they will whisper to those who have a sense of their audience. Of course, you can't know immediately what is whispered about but you will certainly know when those responsible to act, will act on the whispers. *Lekin tab tak bahut der ho chuki hoti hai. Ab pachtake hota kya jab chiriya chun gai khet.* (By then it is too late. It is no use crying over spilt milk.) People normally dub people like you as "nobodies" or "utter failures".' He painted a vividly repellent image of me but I respect him. 'Okay, sir. That, I am.' I was devoid of option. Given Professor Yadav's vast experience in the field of education where groups and coteries have had a very significant role to play, I felt tempted to ask him as to the mechanics of the coterie and how it controls powerful people. Professor Yadav shared his experience thus, "There, once upon a time, was a great virtuous, old, prince charming holding a high position in an educational institution. Fondly we used to call him Mr Rangilla because of his habits that I will enumerate for you. He was tall, gaunt and normally haggard-looking, with grey hair, and a cadaverous face—dry and long—like a broken drum. Fond of flaunting his anger everywhere and a self-styled paragon of virtue, well aware of the idiosyncrasies of the enemy called "old age", he took extreme precautions to fight it with the help of his own idiosyncrasies. Early morning, he would eat seven almonds soaked in water; during the night, he took vitamin and mineral supplements, went for regular walks, used ripe papaya pulp on his face for rejuvenation, and if rumours were to be believed, frequented a quaint known for prescribing ointments for strengthening inner nerves. He believed in having internal health. So, he not only opened himself to all methods of improving it, but took upon himself the responsibility for correcting any deficiency in others, whosoever he/she might be. His generosity in observing women of all ages meticulously and a genuine appreciation for younger ones was remarkable. He was around sixty-seven years old and he compensated that by donning clothes like that of a young man of thirty. The air of authority drew a number of women around him—something he relished much. His obsession was with numbers and names.

Two women were privy to his deeds. One of them, Honeymoon madam, never oblivious to her functional and territorial jurisdiction, was always on guard and as a part of it, generally placed herself at a very uncomfortable distance from him. People had many theories about it. Some suspected she did it to keep a close watch on him so that she could mark any deviation he exuded in favour of some other woman of inconsequence. Others suspected she did it to explore him further for further exploitation. She knew his one weakness and he had many. The other of the two was already suspected to be knocking at the door. Honeymoon madam was very alert; she did not want to lose the battle which she had held for quite some time. The end was approaching fast and the mere prospect of it was too frightening for both Honeymoon madam and her mentor.'

'But sir, how will you interpret people like him who prefer to be controlled by a group or a coterie. What are their features? I am more interested in that,' I asked Professor Yadav.

'Let me confront you with this passage from Fyodor Dostoevsky's *Notes from Underground*:

> "Man really is stupid, phenomenally stupid. That is, he's by means stupid, but rather he's so ungrateful that it would be hard to find the likes of him. I, for example, would not be the least bit surprised if suddenly, out of the blue, amid future reasonableness, some gentleman of ignoble, or, better, of retrograde and jeering physiognomy, should emerge, set his arms akimbo, and say to us all: well, gentlemen, why don't we reduce all this reasonableness to dust with one good kick, for the whole purpose of sending all these logarithms to the devil and living once more according to our own stupid will. That would still be nothing, but what is offensive is that he'd be sure to find followers: that's how man is arranged."

Then, for my benefit, Professor Yadav analysed this passage to portray some features of such persons prone to be controlled by coteries:

1. Such men are ungrateful, though if you believe Dostoevsky, man is phenomenally stupid.
2. Such men are ignoble men using coterie's stupidity.
3. Such men do not set their arms akimbo but raise and move these as if a megalomaniac is fighting with unseen fears.
4. They are past masters in reducing reasonableness to dust: only they matter.

5. They are ruthless kickers with no regard for others' emotional equilibrium.
6. They happen to be men whom fortune favours with stupid followers.

'All these groups and coteries and all those nurturing them must remember one thing. One can fool a few people for some time but one cannot fool everyone all the time. Persons like Mr Rangilla and Honeymoon madam will invariably get exposed one day.'

Professor Yadav's parting words still echo in my ears.

(III)

Professor Yadav was a professor of economics but he was fond of what he used to call 'the greatest trio with the most knotty minds'—Hardy, Borges and Beckett, and relished talking about them. He would often say, 'If you want to live really in current times, read these gentlemen. They will help you die sagaciously.' But today, as I found myself looking at his tired face, he asked me,

'KK, have you ever dared to look at the face of Samuel Beckett?'

'Why dare? Yeah, I have.'

'Have you noticed something there?'

'Where? There.'

'His face—his pictures.'

'No. I think it is a sample face of those destined to think and then write, again think and again write. And then doomed to die.'

'All right. But think of me—what I feel of him. I look at Beckett's face and two things strike me the most: he is nowhere there and he is there everywhere.'

'Sir, you say the same thing of Borges and Hardy.'

'The trio. Their tolerance was superb. You have to be tolerant to be a writer. A writer suffers in the usurping hands of arguments. A writer has to tolerate the burden of arguments. Arguments are the greatest usurpers.'

'Oh, I see. Sir, can we convert the conversation to the Indian scenario where the current debate on intolerance is on the rise? See what the hell is happening out there on the roads, streets, TV channels and the corridors of power.'

'KK, now you see for yourself how relevant that genius playwright is to our Indian society today? These useless fellows attacking a brave order: an order meant to correct decades-old infirmities are talking utter nonsense.' Professor Yadav seemed very agitated but continued, 'Dissent and disagreement have been a part of our cultural, literary, intellectual and historical inheritance. Ours is a democracy. We have every place for civilized arguments and equally civilized counterarguments—these are the hallmarks of democratic functioning.'

'But sir, imagine these don't exist then...' I had started taking an interest in Professor Yadav's pronouncements.

'Then you will be missing something important. You will miss the possibility of ideas—new ideas. There wouldn't be a possibility to modify ideas or improve these. Tell me what will stop the untrammeled growth of undesirable ideas?'

'Sir, I read somewhere: there sleeps a danger—the danger of arguments and dissent acting as maiming agents. What do you think?'

Professor Yadav looked grimmer than usual and then he spoke,

'Think of another scene. You place the arguments in wrongly motivated hands, who are not given to playing the games democracy dictates. And see the magic. These can cause serious fissures even in the most healthiest fabric of a nation's life. Who the hell is interested in genuine and elegant points of view? Juvenile, cynical, immature and lopsided considerations guide the noisy people. One loses sight of the more serious issues a society encounters. Let me give practical wisdom to you, KK. For instance, some crazy group might argue why the ideas already in existence should continue and why these should not be tampered with. See recent happenings and demonstrations against so called intolerance in various parts in the country particularly Delhi. These buggers' inculcated-dissent is founded on grudging assumptions. Nobody is a fool. Former rulers portray arrogance and ignorance. They try to usurp illogic and dispense with logic.'

I told Professor Yadav how in the first week of May 2014, I had reviewed Narendra Modi's (he was not the prime minister then) book of poetry—*A Journey*—and sent it to a foreign literary journal whose chief editor happened to be a Muslim gentleman and a friend. His initial gusto to publish this review waned within a week. Perhaps because this literary review did not meet the literary ethos of his journal. Here is a case of passion taking precedence over everything else.

Professor Yadav heard me, left and came back after ten minutes with a thin book in his hands. The title of the book read—*Watt*, a novel by Samuel Beckett. 'KK, I am sure you have not read it. Do spend some time with it and then I will let you know where your ignorance lies. But come after a week or two and then we will talk.' As I was about to leave, he came nearer to me and hummed, 'Sometimes you should read unappealing books. The books which readers of the current era don't even remember, don't know. Every Tom, Dick, Harry is reading bestselling authors. Or at least claiming to read them. See idiocy of human intellect in those boxes. These books are already concluded ones. Never read contemporary books. They contain shit every contemporary writer is wallowing in. These books represent decadence of intellect. Forget them. Read this book. See inside. See arbitrariness of ascending minds. You stand face to face with Mephistopheles.'

One day, Professor Yadav asked me a straight question, 'Could you understand *Watt* and can you apply it to that Muslim editor's behaviour towards our Prime Minister Narendra Modi's book whose review you attempted?' Without waiting for a response from me, though I admit I was least prepared for a question of this magnitude from my teacher, Professor Yadav breathed heavily and allowed some wisdom to accumulate on his sagging face before he said, 'KK, this bloody history is a great fucker. It fucks every time you confront it with a question. This is okay. But, in a vast country like ours there is not one question or two. Our history has a plethora of questions. Many of these are buried. All deep, dense and difficult questions. These are the questions that are never dead and these peek out intermittently. Almost the entire history of our nation is replete with questions.'

'Absolutely sir. But, sir, don't you feel these require serious debates and discussions,' I could not resist offering a viewpoint which Professor Yadav did not relish much.

'You interrupt a lot. Behave yourself. I was coming to that. Let us talk about current hiccups and not tiny things. But who is there to discuss? You mean these bloody weighty and high-pitched monologues on TV channels? Some of these anchors are greatest liabilities for our eyes and ears. They aggravate tensions. They act like atypical antipsychotic drugs leaving viewers with life-long side effects.'

'Sir, but there are still ignoramuses galore questioning the Vedas and Hindu scriptures. Can you discuss serious issues with them?' I interrupted again, 'What about nationalism, dissent and the reluctance to listen? See how hackneyed the trend has become? Every second intellectual is farting aloud...' I felt the joy of my spoken words. Professor Yadav smiled meekly. He never laughed, never smiled broadly. He went on,

'No harm in farting aloud. What else these so-called intellectuals do? They walk with others' wives and others walk with their wives. All these wives prefer that. But, now a serious point.'

'Sir,' I said.

'Listen. In Terence's play *Andria*, you have a character named Davus. This fellow suffered deep-rooted reluctance to confront difficult questions. He distinguished himself from Oedipus who solved the riddle of sphinx. Beckett coined a term "Davus complex" to describe those who evade difficult questions. This is the point I was driving home...' Professor Yadav seemed to be addressing students in a class room. He continued, 'Past is inevitable. The issues plaguing the present are serious. There is no shying away. Where are genuine minds? There is a climate of suspicion. These suspecting chaps possess the "Davus complex". Many of them fumble while facing even very simple questions. Many fragments of history need reciprocal treatment. Can you open *Watt*?'

I did; he took the book and allowed it to slip into his coarse hands. All in a mechanical way. Rushed through some pages and then asked me to read carefully three portions from three pages respectively—the underlined ones. He had already underlined these in dark yellow. Professor Yadav liked yellow; he used to be swayed by its calming effect.

The three tiny, crisp excerpts:

'What rubbish,' said the gentleman.
'What nonsense,' said the lady.

And sometimes Watt understood all, and sometimes he understood much, and sometimes he understood little, and sometimes he understood nothing.

'Officer,' he cried, 'as God is my witness, he had his hand upon it.
God is a witness that cannot be sworn.'

'I have read, sir. What next?' I must admit that I didn't understand why Professor Yadav drew my attention to these three unrelated excerpts at all.

'And you ask me what next. History has many broken parts. Those interested in debates and discussions on intolerance must first know this. How to address such broken parts? They don't do that. Solemnly they prefer to mimic that peculiar but easy to follow method of argumentative pronouncements from *Watt*. I mean the three excerpts.'

'Sorry, sir. Could I ask for a little more clarity on the issue?'

'Wisdom on the decline, KK, isn't it? There is every possibility that a dialogue based on concealment of ambivalent feelings would lead to a fragmented dialogue. Like the one between the gentleman and the lady above. And the two arguers would land in a situation where both of them, like Watt, "understood nothing". A complete impasse awaits both.'

'Oh I see. That's the tragic end. No public understanding, no harmony in such discussions. These lead to turmoil and chaos.' I was happy that I had been able to understand him.

'And also absurdity as in *Watt*. Reasoned arguments are dead arguments,' Professor Yadav uttered lowly.

'Why, sir?'

'See, there are causes of failure of reasoned cultivation of understanding and persuasive techniques. The type of dialogues we have here, I abhor. I know of scholars pointing out the difficulty people engaged in dialogues and discussions have.' Professor Yadav looked aghast and jaded.

'Is it their inability to accept the authenticity of the version of self the other person puts forth?' I tried to divert Professor Yadav's attention from his fatigue. But he was a different man altogether when amidst such conversations.

'That is not the point. Even though what you put forward is

a true reflection of your inner reality, distortions creep in filtering your inner reality. So to cope with this, I will create a subjective version of your personality. And you will do the same thing for me. Not without benefit. It has one distinct advantage. This way both our inner selves will be revised to reach newness which will be superior to the earlier version. I hope you understand it.'

Before I could react, I heard more from him.

'The problem of bizarreness as in *Watt* is a resolvable problem. Okay, even in the context of situations underway here in India.' Professor Yadav sounded unusually optimistic.

∽

Impressed with Professor Yadav's fabulous capacity to apply what he gleaned from what he had read to current events in our country, I could not help but send him a brief note stating my opinions:

'Analysts are of great service to mankind when they leave behind things that have great relevance in the context of contemporary happenings and it is time for some to learn lessons from literary geniuses like Beckett. Ignorance of history or drawing wrong inferences having no justification from it will fill what is normal with what is really bizarre. The need is to confront questions not addressed or not addressed properly thus far and seek a resolution for a better, wholesome and a matured society to emerge. The present scenario in Indian society, where a new order is shaping up, seems to be conforming to this.'

'So gentleman, here you are. Buck up. Buck up'—Professor Yadav's SMS came today, possibly as a token of appreciation for me or I so suppose.

(IV)

I finished reading *She Will Build Him a City*. The author is

Raj Kamal Jha. A note on the author tells of his present occupation and place of residence. He lives in Gurgaon and works in New Delhi. He further enlightens how being employed as the chief editor of a well-known newspaper affords him 'that rare freedom to drift away when there's an extra tug in the wind.' Two Man Booker Prize shortlisted authors choose to stand as guarantor of this work—their crisp epitomization speaks volumes of their visionary qualities. After all, the guarantor must have some standing in the market. The borrower must be assured and reassured. Metros like Delhi are superimposed models of poverty and affluence like box diagrams in economics. Once a box gets superimposed over another box, people inside get sandwiched. Jha's book is a book about people living inside superimposed boxes where everything is in movement with huge stagnating shadows: 'He raises his hand, just an inch or so, to check if he can move.'

Jha, master sculptor, takes humdrum life of a Man, a Woman and a Child with their pseudo-civilized characteristics and transports readers to a realm where all the three bring forth shockingly delineated art from unfathomable sources making it an intellectually engrossing work. Time, love and its absence, past and its resonance, alienation and a sense of dooming extinction are the hovering themes in this book which propels itself on disjointedness—considerable disjointedness in terms of 'what we see, what we touch and what we hear'—a phrase from French philosopher, Henri Bergson who Jha fondly remembers and who enables Jha to 'sprinkle visual dust all around' against the otherwise well spread-out 'darkest hour.' To understand Jha's 'She' who will build 'Him', a 'City', one has to live, a la Bergson, 'outside of oneself'.

A threadbare and true pasteurization of typical modern day society with all kinds of diversities: life in the slums, the lavishness of the affluent who have no reluctance or inhibitions in squandering huge sums of money to have fun or a change from the monotony of daily routine life at home in exchange for a mere luxury of a night at a star hotel, the day-to-day miseries of the lowest strata of the society, the frustrations of middle- and upper-middle class working men and women, the boisterous lifestyles of children and teenagers of the upper and most affluent in society, the perversions of the meanest kind, extramarital relations that thrive under conducive circumstances of modern day lifestyles, aspirations in the guise of service and efficiency that underlie the actions of bureaucrats, false disguises aimed solely at satisfying egos—all these themes and more find space in this tale of modern India where, 'She cannot understand what he says because he speaks a language she has never heard.' This is the beauty of true India.

The passageway to Jha's consciousness is blocked by rocks, his imagination conveniently puts forward, obscurely securing unlimited access to truths which he has gathered from reading other literature. Salman Rushdie exorcises his readers through the linguistic complexity that he employs to reach the contents of his ruminations. Jha, on the other hand, simplifies facts and fiction in a way his reader adopts these as reflections of his own images. But then Jha leaves his readers in a quandary: 'Where does he get his remarkable images from? Well that's a mystery...' Yeah. Great novelists love to toy with mysteries. Jha has a deep sense of seclusion. Seclusion and mystery make excellent bedfellows.

In the course of his narration, the author resorts to the use of a few symbols and frames to give life to his thoughts. In between a few frames, seemingly having no semblance or relevance to the natural hop from one frame to another, something has crept in, causing, sometimes, a feeling of a faltering step or straying off-route. This leaves the reader pondering; just pondering why the remarks from the scientist from Brisbane—'life expectancy for people with Down's syndrome is steadily going up'—are 'welcomed with thunderous applause.' Here one watches the contradiction between perils of Down's syndrome and increasing life expectancy. Jha's book is about the linkages. His novel proceeds on linkages though jumbled ones.

A reviewer does not look through the windows of other houses; he has his own windows. But disputants argue that the best reviewers never look through their windows; they choose others' windows to kill the bird. Now, let Edward Albee, the American playwright, come to the scene. I feel Albee is one writer who comes very close to Jha, in as much as Jha, like Albee, weds realism of modern life of the streets of Delhi and Gurgaon with philosophical orientations of his mind: something Albee has done in his *The Zoo Story*. It's only this that peeps from behind the curtains of linguistic contrivance these two genius writers are so apt at.

'But that's the way the cookie crumbles.' Jerry's pragmatism is lucid.

While talking of the superimposed world of livelihood, both Albee and Jha exist in their writings in terms of their personal relationships—with the ideas they impose on to others, their notions as to what makes the narrative easy and worth having a look at. But still the unknowable utters. Failure to understand what our deepest desires dictate us to know leads writers to the jarring realization of the unavoidable. Albee introducing his readers to Jerry's lousy rooming-house, the death of his parents (Jerry's parents died when he was 'ten-and-a-half-years old'), his attempt to poison a drunken woman's dog though unsuccessfully, his distasteful neighbours are like Jha introducing his readers to the messy and fragmented stories of Man, Woman and Child, the stories that are never resolved.

However, off and on one gets some vivid glimpses of a genuinely open and caring mentality of a middle-class family, where there still exist strong family bonds, very rare in this age of modern independent living and also the undisguised sincerity and open-mindedness of dwellers in the distant and remote villages where the pretences of city life have not succeeded as yet in corrupting the basic characters of the innocent and plain villagers.

The rickshaw-wallah and his family who live in the slum from which also hails the maid of the orphanage, the flashy TV anchor, the loving father who, having no fridge in his house, goes out to bring some raw ice to make cool drinks for his little daughter, etc., are all lifelike characters one comes across in everyday life giving space, at times, to some very fine nostalgic memories of a common and lovable ordinary household. A lot of characters come and go in between; a few stay till the end.

Balloon Girl, Orphan, the street dog 'Bhow', the sub-human character living in the darkness of the theatre in the Mall, 'the 18 inches long, just under 10 inches wide, the size of a small cat' cockroach in the swimming pool, the 12 feet tall woman figure (who elicits a question to Ma, 'how do we go about looking for her?' to which Ma replies, 'Don't you worry. I say, we will meet her... Because how can you keep someone so tall hidden for so long?') who comes to carry you away in your sleep, etc., are a few of the symbols Jha has used successfully to bridge the gap between fiction and reality, leaving much to the readers' speculation and imagination.

On YouTube, in his conversation with another author Vu Tran, Jha attributes the birth of this book to, 'Thinking of it—what you do when there is despair'. And he said a very interesting thing, 'You can build yourself a city in your head but what if you cannot?' The water bottle lay on the table, unused throughout. The book is a book to be built in the head, but what if you cannot?

Let me now turn to thoughts Jha places before his readers. Jha's handling of many thoughts puts a reader on varying plateaus affording him an opportunity to look at time from different complex dimensions that are not easily accessible to his perceptual process. Time is not an imaginary entity. It is a continual palpitation of moments. The author only conveys some hints and places pointers and leaves meaningful suggestions: 'And he takes a U-turn at the next red light, heads back to AIIMS, he needs to check the mortuary.' Or, on not finding the body: "That's good news then, whoever you came to look for is alive," laughs Mortuary Man.' Jha lets the show reveal and unreel itself in the minds of the reader.

There are thoughts—flat and deep, rich with time or destitute of time. It is a curious phenomenon. In his book, time is a character like any other character—a lighthouse with periodic flashes. When the light accepts it, it shines, when it is rejected, it falls in the quagmire of obscurity. Jha is conscious of himself being reflected in seeking metamorphosis. A great writer is one who does not tiptoe vagaries of time, ideas, memories and words. Rather, he creates his own world of ideas, words amid memories, and superimposes on that world, vagaries of time. Endeavouring to find unhackneyed meaning into the most rotten stuff that makes life—this novel is all about the art of living amidst dinginess.

Then Jha finds within the pause that takes place between the end and the beginning of thought, a sort of swarming. Ailing thoughts lumped together inevitably result in extension of boundaries of psychological symbols of social life. The paths of association delimit the main path itself. And when Jha tries to bring to fruition what foreshadows his malignance and mockery, he provides a glimpse of enclosed characters suspended in mid-air: 'He wants to sleep in the bed in which Balloon Girl and her mother slept. He undresses.' Purging the mind of the sunset, the life of the ephemera does not respond directly and forgotten fragments ultimately result in the blurred experiences.

Both Jha and Albee are linguistically simple but thematically highly complex, highlighting the purposelessness of human behaviour and existence as nothing is expected to occur ever.

The book is likely to be rated as a masterpiece in its own class and breed. This work has depth and demands readership also with an inner perspective capable of delving deep into the subject with creative and imaginative minds to grasp the whole of the impact the author aims at conveying. While both Albee and Jha concern themselves with unmet desires, wants, callousness and stupidity, Jha has one more dimension: he emphasizes on the value of falling man and of magic, it relieves the underprivileged from their pain. 'The capsules work like magic. Ten minutes, the pain is gone.'

Life never gets filled, for we, human beings, have nothing to fill it with. Life is like, to use Jha's words, 'a pale dot of lifeless light'. Life as portrayed by Albee and Jha is like two of Albee's Jerry's empty picture frames:

Peter: About those two empty picture frames…?

Jerry: I don't see why they need any explanation at all. Is it not clear? I don't have pictures of anyone to put in them.

She Will Build Him a City is about empty picture frames: it expects readers to place pictures in the frames. Readers have a choice—to fill the frames or not. Will they ever exercise that choice? Only readers would know that. For the present, a classy book indeed.

(V)

'Wotan'.

The link?

The charming lady who interviewed me for a TV channel about life and literature reminded me at least three times of Carl Jung in a course of forty minutes. 'You seem to have been greatly influenced by Jung, more than Adler and Kurt Lewin though there are traces of their influence in your writings. I am asking you particularly when nowadays, modern Indian writers rarely read these theorists and are more influenced by likes of... Okay let me not take names. You must be aware of these Indian writers writing in English and turning out to be bestselling novelists. Believe me, they are no better than some of the best writers writing crime thrillers in Hindi and whose novels flourish in bookstalls at railway platforms. Many men, while engrossed in hurriedly eating puri-bhaji at railway platforms, would be seen buying these books before they board trains. For just passing time, you know. Anyway, both writers share one common fortune: both have been bestsellers.' While her question, no more than her opinion, was a baffling one in as much as I have read Adler reasonably well, Lewin—his theory of personality—partially, and Jung in passing, I must thank her for arousing my curiosity in the writings of Jung. I am still at a loss with why such a curiosity could not pop up in case of the other two gentlemen whose names she mentioned. Dante gave a clue as to such questions and more relevantly to answers that ought to ensue. So why should I bang my head against a wall which has no piquancy? Dante was vivid with pleasure when asked, 'Why is it that people prefer to interact with buffoons rather than with you?' Pat came the reply, 'Because like likes like.' So that's it.

Jung's essays, this one having a distinction as it talks of things so relevant today, move his readers into a collective psyche of humanity to enable them to get a clearer picture of events around them. What arrested me in this essay was not something I found in it but in another essay titled, 'The Fight With the Shadow' where Jung painstakingly drove home the point that 'psychopathology of the masses is rooted in the psychology of the individual. Only if one succeeds in establishing that certain phenomena or symptoms are common to a number of different individuals can one begin to examine the analogous mass phenomena.' So true.

But now, the real pudding. It lies not in 'The Flight With the Shadow' but in another and certainly more imperious essay titled, 'Wotan'. In my first reading, I found the name quite instilling though as I made headway with this essay, it was a great treasure of thoughts and its applicability to current happenings was in full order. The quiescence of 'ancient god of storm and frenzy', Wotan was not as important as its waking up 'like an extinct volcano'. Jung described Wotan as a restless wanderer hell-bent on creating restlessness and strife through whatever he did. The ugly movements involving thousands of people, like in the German Youth Movement, involved the wanderer Wotan: 'It is an elemental Dionysus breaking into the Apolonian order.' There are times this unique creature rolls on unchecked 'like a rock crashing down the side of a hill until it is stopped by an obstacle stronger than itself'.

Hey presto: here in our land, not one, but many Wotans have awakened. Their hibernation period has passed. They need fresh blood for survival. So they are out, on the roads. That group of literary legends: the dreamers of all sorts of dreams of imperfections and perfections, hell-bent on returning their Sahitya Akademi Awards are moving in tandem to place the wreath at the doors of the Akademi. These refined forms of Wotan, though imprisoned in the deadwood of their own creations, obviously refuse to look at a wider world. For them, this wider world represents an alien society. They refuse to swallow their stridence and disingenuousness. They are totally debilitating, unable to give due respect to the newly and duly elected regime. Our Wotans do not like change; they like turbulence for their survival.

Enough is enough. Institutions like Sahitya Akedemi perform the best when they take rest, but when a few miscreants disturb them necessitating their movement out of their rest, images of the disturbed gait of corpses are the first to invade. Sometimes art and literature can be a knavish business. It hardly takes anything to stir the pot again and a la William Faulkner, 'If a writer is to rob his mother, he will not hesitate; the "Ode on a Grecian Urn" is worth any number of old ladies.' Let me have a look at these literary legends. Yes, a few of them, not necessarily legends in the true sense of the term, get literary awards—a sort of recognition for the creation they bestow on the society. No problem, but what is the role stimulants have in their perceived success? Many literary works may owe their existence to a series of stimulants to enable them to stay when the mirror turns convex. Many of these are in the league of the ilk in late evening socio-literary gatherings where, along with imported scotch, flow lopsided debates about the astounding merits of a newly-released book by the host authors. It's in such a gathering that a bureaucrat acquaintance and fiction writer once quipped, 'You are hardly visible. How often do you circulate? Remember, it pays.' Yeah. Unfortunately, visibility constitutes the sine qua non even for a writer who wishes his 'creativity' to be 'awarded'. Sometimes, reclusiveness steals the thunder but that is really rare. What I have been seeing now adds to my chagrin. There is no dearth of literary luminaries who add to their own vulnerability by using awards as a double-edged weapon in their hands: to keep basking in the limelight off and on and then look forward to have an auspicious occasion to get fresh recognition by relinquishing the awards. Some of the past masters fight repulsive battles in the name of literary awards to get these and some of them—that rare breed skilled in the art of sticking their necks out the second time when it is least needed—pave the way for more battles. If nothing else, returning the award—an attempt by long-waning faces to revive themselves—sells at least temporarily. Public amnesia is curable. Ignition of unwanted and superfluous controversies is a sure cure for it.

The most trustworthy friend is zero. Truth peeps out through zero—a big zero. 'If you look at zero you see nothing; but look through it and you will see the world.' That is Robert Kaplan and that is his baiting book *The Nothing That Is*. This book gives good lessons for literary luminaries. Kaplan is not only a great rescuer but also a great retriever who rescues these literary luminaries—men and women of extraordinary perception and intuition, the self-styled epitomes of honesty, intelligence and sophistry—from the vagaries of their self-evolved imbalances. Much of their problems arise from their propensity to look at the zero and zero alone and retrieve imaginary fears from the ecstasy of such imbalances. They have come to pass when they should start looking at events through the zero. Only then would they be freed of the idea that emanates not only from their basking in the limelight, but also from the delusions of grandeur about their creativity and its recognition. One ought not to lull oneself with the theory that 'awards are supreme'. These are not if wedded to certain ideologies or power systems. And never forget there are believers that many of the literary awards have their own stories of drama, intrigue and treachery.

Awards do confer on awardees recognition and publicity and make them an inseparable part of literary academies. The power to accept the award does not confer on the awardees the power to relinquish it later, for the recognition and publicity that go with such awards are irreversible and there are none to take the awards back. One's disinclination to accept any award must be exhibited once one is called upon to accept it. Becoming wiser later may be petrifying and people would be tempted to read between the lines: a possible red herring.

But, who are these revered luminaries? What is needed is a careful look at the luminaries who chanced upon and quickly gripped an auspicious occasion to avail themselves of the luxury to relinquish the awards thus bamboozling onlookers like me. Many of these luminaries may seem to belong to 'literary groups based on ideology and literary preferences' and may be at a loss to accept an ideology which for them and their followers might seem to be an anathema. Then there is a group, albeit a tiny one, whose allegiance to a power system is known far afield. Some of these generous relinquishes have been dominating Sahitya Akademi for years influencing its decisions and milking it as and when required. A new regime is in place and any newness in the writing on the wall may be unnerving for some. When books create controversy, it is welcome and the magnificent grandeur of art lies in justifying and accepting all such controversies. The real problem arises when writers create controversies and generously gift themselves the honour to wallow in these. Foreign newspapers that consider it infra dig to talk of literary prizes lesser than Nobel and Booker and literary mortals lesser than Salman Rushdie have suddenly started talking eloquently about the Sahitya Akademi writers who relinquish awards. While a writer may not dethrone his carefully crafted ideology in his writings, he may allow it to play the secondary role. Let the tree be the tree and its shadow a shadow. Literature does not thrive on ideology alone and a writer's literary maturity thrives as much on his hindsight as on his foresight.

Writers must neither live in glass houses nor make castles in the air. But our award-relinquishing writers do both.

(VI)

I realize there is an edginess about the title of this chapter; it has a form that's jagged. There are strings not tied in adequately.

There might be discontinuities of the narrative here, but these very discontinuities redeem themselves justifying the rationale behind the strong relationship obtaining between authors, books and some elements of human nature that are depicted in them. The analytical approach to examination of logic underlying a particular behaviour serves at least one purpose: it leaves a scope for a madman of yesterday becoming a genius of today or vice versa. It is all about engaged skepticism and continual subjecting of 'doubts' to probing by minds capable of not playing to the gallery and thus looking beyond the horizon. These minds never mope; they survive the worst, they rest their hopes in 'doubts' becoming less hazy with the passage of time.

CHAPTER 10

Of Social Niceties

(I)

'Fame is like a beautiful woman; the more you chase it, the more it will elude you,' I told the lady TV interviewer who concealed her expressions with considerable success and then I heard her very soft, inaudible voice saying 'Thanks.' I had succeeded in passing the test of social nicety that day.

(II)

Knotting the tie is and has always been a headache for me. I had received this tie three years back on my wedding anniversary from my neighbour who was settled in some country abroad. He, from each of his visits to his town, brings gifts and distributes them lavishly as a mark of his fabulous lifestyle abroad. He hires the most expensive taxis: not ones like ambassador, fiat or a maruti van, but air-conditioned taxis, ones that are good-looking, chauffeur-driven, and have dark, tinted glasses.

The tie he brought for me is perceived to be a unique one,

especially in the small town I was living in. I had determined to wear it on occasions I considered important. Today, I've put it on since it's an inaugural session of an important course on 'Gender Matters in Higher Bureaucracy' for acclimatizing participants to women empowerment.

'Put it on only when you are wearing a white shirt,' my neighbour had pointed out, his opinion indicative of the superb skills only fashion designers of today can boast of. 'Match it with a black trouser. If you don't have it, grey would also do. But avoid any other colour.'

'If you don't have one...'—I mark his words. Yes, I don't have one: he knows it.

'I am not so fussy about how a man should dress himself,' I say looking at the tie, the glittering tie.

'That is the precise reason you are looked down upon in the parties you go. You bring shame to me. Disgraceful,' my wife says. Good clothes contribute to the personality. A man looks elegant and intelligent in good clothes.

'Look at the others. How did they manage to stay at two or three stations? Go and meet them; ask them about their art,' my wife says with pity while she combs her hair and is in the process of removing dandruff.

The Authority. No one has seen him; no one has met him. Someone has camouflaged him. Who is this someone? Is it one entity, a living human being or a group of three to five persons? A coterie?

Some representations have no values; these are predestined. A superannuated bureaucrat who suffered in the hands of the coterie, was fond of sharing his worldly wisdom, 'Don't think of making representations. Bosses are past masters in filing representations of those they don't like. They simply file some for the present. And in bureaucracy, future never comes. Manage things verbally.

Just put in a word in time to the persons who matter. The coterie. Best be part of the coterie and if you cannot, then at least be on very good terms with it. You ought to know the way the system works. Go along with the wind; never against it.'

(III)

Mumbai: June 2012, 11th floor of the tower, House number 1101.

I met him after years. It was a lavish dinner party. Mr Verma, a senior executive in a private firm, had organized one to celebrate the 'successful married life' of thirty years.

Although not a fit topic of discussion given the occasion, I felt tempted to ask another 'sir', a highly placed gentleman in bureaucracy, why Sir Thomas More's *Utopia* had become so relevant in modern times, particularly in the context of the functioning of bureaucracy in India and elsewhere. What came my way were his skewed expressions and reply, 'Let me correct you. Demi Moore is an actress and may have no faith in utopia. Actresses don't believe in utopia. Enjoy the party, man.'

Good heavens.

'Do you visit parties? Go to the places these parties are organized in.' Ms Kumar, a woman of fifty-five, trying to look gorgeous but pitiably failing in it, looked upon these parties as an avenue to discharge her frustrations and more importantly, add to her husband's.

'How are you, madam?' I said. 'I must confess you are looking far more beautiful and charming than ever before. I am really sorry for having missed your marriage anniversary last month. People still talk about it.'

'Thank you very much. So sweet of you. But I trust what you have voiced is true in letter and spirit. Of course, you talk turkey, as Americans use this word. Still it's better to confirm it. I normally have a distaste for the right things not being said rightly,' her response was not unexpected as she was known for mistrusting genuine words of appreciation.

'Absolutely. I believe in good utterances. Only men of vision would doubt them.'

'You mean women have no sense of vision?'

I never expected this reaction. I said, 'I feel your doubts are unwarranted, madam.'

Ms Kumar was apparently annoyed with what she thought was an insipid observation. 'I feel sorry about this deviation. But look at different places around you and you wouldn't miss the tragedy. So many people eulogized for the virtues they themselves think they don't possess.' The party continued. Ms Kumar moved on. Cocktail.

(IV)

'Tomorrow, 12.40 sharp.' My appointment with Mr Verma was ultimately fixed. 'Mr Verma has an important meeting at one. So please be on time,' I was told.

'Meeting at one? Lunch time starts then,' I asked. The principal private secretary smiled.

Mr Verma had joined his new assignment a week back but his predecessor, being busy in some important work, agreed with Mr Verma that he takes over a week later.

Mr Verma was given a room in a tall tower in Mumbai other than the one his predecessor was occupying. He was waiting to be moved to a bigger room. He did not relish it.

Mr Verma had a penchant for being in the company of women and his late-night parties. He made an excellent host. His only problem was insomnia and the sleep-inducing drugs had no impact on him. Even heavy drinks were of no use. He had started taking oil baths just before going to bed but in vain. He hated being initiated into any serious discussions about books and authors. He had an average knowledge of his work content but he had an awesome reputation among his seniors as well as juniors of being an upright and savvy person.

His wife was attractive and generally believed to be liberal-minded much like her husband. She was known not only for her interest in cookery but also her efforts towards imparting awareness about gender sensitivity among men. She raised funds for her NGO courtesy the benevolence of her powerful husband.

I arrive to meet Mr Verma five minutes earlier than the time appointed. The principal private secretary looks first at me, then at the wall clock. 'Another five minutes,' she says. She then busies herself with a photo album. It is 12.40 on the clock and she informs Mr Verma of my presence and signals me towards the door. I enter Mr Verma's office. A local movie or serial titled 'Hamar Ghunghatwa Zaldi Uthawa' (Lift my veil quickly) is playing on the television. He asks, 'Have we met earlier? I don't think so.' He is right. He didn't seem very much at ease with strangers and I was one at that time. He was from the illustrious St Stephen's College in Delhi. Mr Verma had a psychic turmoil: he feared being shown his true self in his own face which he had hidden from strangers like me, from small towns, and which men and women of his ilk shared abundantly with him.

A few of his friends fondly justify Mrs Verma's attitude keeping Proust's Countess in mind: 'She is exclusive, she only meets people of blue blood.' Where so, then, do small town persons like me stand a chance? Considered to be an expert on European cuisine, she relishes tea from the earthen cup praising the 'desi' style of drinking tea. When in her 'moods', Mrs Verma smokes too but that's a rarity. 'Occasionally, you know.'

Many of these eulogies smack of incongruities. Tarred. They are so jarring, so deceptive as to put any one of salt to shame. Kakku Jain, a junior bureaucrat, teetotaller by birth and a deeply religious person. Jain sought what he preferred one to call 'Mr Verma's kind permission' to allow him to participate in the discussion. Jain's attitude was noticeable everywhere but more particularly in parties that lasted till near dawn. Mr Verma was more than welcoming of Jain's opinions; his acknowledgements clearly weren't reserved only for women. Jain had also recently arranged for Mr Verma and his wife's trips abroad. So the encouragement to engage Jain in conversations during the recent party was almost like returning the courtesy, an end to which he proved to be more obliging than necessary.

Kakku Jain had an uncle. Superannuated a few years back. You know, uncles really matter in bureaucratic jobs. 'These uncles ensure smooth elevation. If you don't have an uncle in bureaucracy, then be ready to be screwed each time you are not liked. And in equal measure.' The same senior bureaucrat identifying Sir Thomas More with Demi Moore was conferring, I recollect distinctly, with yet another senior bureaucrat in the Secretariat café last evening. He was whispering and no guesses for that. On the other side, Mrs Verma was recollecting memories from her last tour, 'Oh! The trip was wonderful,' and she guided herself towards the cocktail table. Kakku Jain tiptoed behind. Good bureaucrats know the art of tiptoeing. They inherit this art from better and more experienced bureaucrats.

Now my soliloquy: Many, after having passed a one-time examination, decide to twist themselves into knots to make sure all their reading and scholarship go for good. Please remember my confession earlier that with my passing civil services examination, an exalted opinion about my scholarship was established at least for me. Does it not apply to many including the one identifying Sir Thomas More with Demi Moore? These are the men and women who prosper through such parties thrown by the likes of Mr Verma: their gaze is mid-level, they have no large notions, no idea of interiors. Exteriors infatuate them; these bring them face to face with their ilk. That is the precise reason I don't circulate. I wish they could believe the power of words, of words poured out by Vladimir Nabokov, 'Where there is beauty, there is pity, for beauty must die. It dies.' These people, replete with stylized arrogance and a self-eulogized persona, must realize that one day their stylized arrogance and self-eulogized persona will die.

(V)

A bunch of fellow travellers superannuating. Farewell party organized. It was customary to have three speakers who were required to say 'a few words', as a mark of respect for the departing ones. I ventured forth. I write. But I ought to speak, at least some time.

'Ladies and gentlemen. I cannot tell you how grateful I am to our distinguished association for giving me this opportunity to say a few words. Members of our distinguished association deserve great appreciation for the onerous responsibility of furthering the cause of common issues on their shoulders, apart from ensuring their continuation here, at one station.

I did not volunteer but I am here. I am here as a consequence of a search conducted by the secretary of the distinguished association among those present for the third speaker as the lady who spoke first had finished and the second one was on the job. There was, however, a problem. The searchers had laid down a criterion. As a matter of fact, they found one who they thought had all the attributes to satisfy that criterion. That gentleman had to, however, excuse himself because he had a sore throat. I asked a colleague why amongst so many present only this gentleman had been spotted.

He replied, taking the glass of whisky near his lips, "You don't know him. He has massive experience in saying *a few words*. I have seen him in these farewell parties for the last fifteen years saying them. He speaks English very fluently and very loudly. And not only this, he laughs more loudly than he speaks." Clearly, the criterion was, as I realized, Find one who can speak English very fluently and very loudly and laughs more loudly than he speaks intermittently. And they found that gentleman.

'Respected madams and sirs, I admit, I am a failure here. This criterion I cannot satisfy. I can neither speak English very fluently nor very loudly. My being a writer makes me a sluggish thinker. I think before I write. I know how responsibly brains ought to behave. The other day, in a meeting, I heard that short fellow speaking English very loudly, very fluently, conveying virtually nothing. He reminded me of "Folie a' deux", a poem published in my first poetry collection, *Ineluctable Stillness*. A world that imprisons the clash of their restless, piercing egos/vague retrieval/ of numbing convulsions. I have seen many cases of "Folie a' deux" here. So I will think before I speak just like I think before I write. Kindly appreciate my limitation. But I will try to do justice.

To quote a poet, "I have become the evidence." I call upon all of you to become evidence of the present; only then you will see and more importantly show the path to your junior fellow travellers for a brighter future where the collective wisdom will not be called upon to locate a "many timer", well-versed in the art of "speaking fluent English very loudly". This is the summary of my search for my identity amongst you people. Many of you might be thinking and rightly so how hopeless my understanding is. The unsparing, the unsentimental hands that shaped me shaped that rare breed of "many timers", but with a difference. I was bamboozled; while the latter bamboozled the hands that shaped them. In the end, I represent often-tormented realities of the dual relationship while the "many timers" acquire and move into more absurd realm of farce. It is a strange business to love absurdity and shun creativity. Please at least now take my point. Does only spring make history? The world is changing so rapidly and we are at quarrel with ourselves as to when and where to use "what". Bravo. Bravo. We justify ourselves. That is the only truth about us. Our very ethos is guided by intimidations and trepidations. Let us avoid the "holier than thou attitude" that makes us a dodo outside and a bigger dodo inside. Collective mistrust is our strongest force binding us to our core. Our collective existence enlivens us, blossoms us. The day it collapses, our fragile structure will collapse. Thank you all for listening to me silently.'

(VI)

There were none—neither Samuel Taylor Coleridge, nor William Hazlitt nor tavern. Nor James Thomson nor his *The Seasons*. (In a tavern there lay on the window-seat, Thomson's book *The Seasons* giving Coleridge his 'aha' moment propelling him to admit to Hazlitt also present there, 'That is true fame.') But Mr Datta was going to have yet another opportunity to enjoy his aha moment, for his first son's first fiction book, a la Mr Datta had already reached its 'true fame'.

'Frankfurt Airport…have you ever been there?' Mr Datta, a senior position holder in the hierarchy of power and recognized for his astute talents in accomplishing things amoral, asked glancing at none of the six about to occupy their chairs placed around the dining table arranged for 'a courtesy lunch thrown in honour of Mrs and Mr Datta' by one of the leading engineering institutes of which his office was 'the sole examiner'. The six people included Mr and Mrs Datta (roughly fifty-eight years old), their twenty-three-old son, an immediate subordinate of Mr Datta, a lady who was hosting the dinner (may be around forty-five years of age, with thick lips, large eyes, unstrained cheeks, and a muscular body), and myself. Widely known among his colleagues and subordinates for his unstable appetite for things coming his way 'courtesy his being the sole examiner', Mr Datta was loosening his red tie as he cautiously sat his heavy body down on the white soft sofa specially placed for him. Before one could notice the impact of his question, he asked, looking direct into madam's eyes, 'Are you comfortable? Last night she had a tummy upset.' Madam smiled. Sir got the answer and looking at the host introduced his master son, 'Meet Jackey. Doing B.Tech in Noida, but writing a thriller. Expected any time towards the end of the year.' The host seemed to have placed her worries somewhere else but forcing a smile uttered, 'Oh yes, indeed. A novelist in the making.'

Mr Datta was avid in his praise, 'A thriller novelist. His elder brother is already well-known. He has published one book last year and is doing well, really well. I am really happy.' Madam continued with an intense look at the starters being served. 'His opening scene just chilled me. The script is so riveting. It just liberates. It uplifts the reader. What a glorious effusion of language and ideas!' Mr Datta tried hard to fork the marrow from the piece of mutton he was on the verge of eating but it proved a hard nut and he then tried equally hard to remove the fork from the piece. Failing again, he asked for a new fork. When free, he again absorbed everyone's attention in his son's literary grandeurs, 'He could notice illusions in wall paintings, delusions in his father's memories, hallucinations in his morbid desires—his debut novel is all about these and the common space. But he never struggles with his narratives. My son's friend is there. Last week, he telephoned to tell him that he spotted his book on the stalls of the Frankfurt Airport. That's real fame. All bestselling Indian authors are there, on the shelves of the bookstalls at Frankfurt

Airport. Have you ever been to Frankfurt Airport, KK?'

I thought to myself—the vessel contains what the ocean does not and with an uncertain, swindling nod responded to Mr Datta's question. It was as if a corpse was lying by the side of another corpse waiting to be cremated. Ultimately everything ends in a fiasco of a funeral.

Can a writer reach the innermost recesses of a dead man?

(VII)

The bride's face is veiled; none has seen it but the chaps go gaga. Applause doesn't cease—the sound of collectiveness marks the crescendo at a book-release function. Tell me what better comparison you can give. No one has seen the book; it is wrapped in a brown cover with a red ribbon tied around it and the gentleman performing the onerous task of cutting the ribbon and seeing the book is no better than a bridegroom removing the veil of his bride on the first night. I abhor going to any book-reading session, more so a poetry-reading session. I know what happens in these places. A jamboree of unwanted fellows gather, each itching for being heard and in reverence irrespective of whether they have something worthwhile to say or not.

Nothing pains me more than the sight of a poet on the verge of reciting his poems and all genuine poets struggle while hundreds of eyes yawn at them, sometimes mockingly and always unbelievingly. A poet's greatest enemy is his audience—an audience so restless as to be remarkably nonchalant about what is likely to happen in the less than 10 per cent filled hall. Thinness is one issue, absence of fullness another. Both are not the same. You agree. Don't feign you are not listening. I know you are.

But this time I said, let me go. After all, a fellow bureaucrat has invited me. Not that bureaucrats cannot write. They do; what else can they do if not write. Their power lies in their ability to 'draft'. I enjoyed the moments my boss would call me and order—'draft this letter' or 'draft this note' or 'draft this minute' or 'I want this draft in, say, ten minutes' but some bosses tell smilingly, 'I want an error-free draft' or 'make a crisp, short draft but a readable one', or 'I want a detailed draft touching everything important but no wastage. They must understand what I want to convey. Okay. Now go please'. On auspicious occasions like superannuations and transfers, when only good qualities in bureaucrats are suddenly discovered and eulogized upon, it is very common to hear (I hear it with numbing bemusement) colleagues, seniors in particular, recalling how good the superannuated ones' drafting capabilities had been and how the world is now going to miss that. Who will fill in the gaps? The vacuum that yawns with the visage of night growing wider would never be filled. Once a gentleman virtually yelled from the dais, 'I want error-free documents, totally error free, you understand.' The ensuing thunderous applause reminded me of poetess Kamla Das's 'The Dance of Eunuchs'. Yes, not all but most of us have not read Kamla Das. It is another story that that particular gentleman had never read anything and still defended zealously what he had never read or written. His skills lay in defending the most indefensible and every time he did it, his factotums welcomed it; as yet another cliché goes, 'rising to the occasion'. He suffered a disease caused by a virus of overreach. He preferred to act as a bull in a china shop and made a mountainous virtue of eminent qualification of his fading being. And this he did through his manufactured narratives with no basis. What I want to push forward is that bureaucrats can also write; they wield their superior power through the might of the pen they hold in their hands and that they use with remarkable alacrity and piece of mind with terrifying impact as intended.

Some, sometimes, write poetry too.

∽

The chief guest for the occasion was a lady—very fair and very obese—who had to perform a venerable job half an hour later. She was looking into some papers seriously and carrying out some corrections. So it seemed. The dais was full and there were seven people gracing the occasion—three on her left and three on the right side.

That beautiful, thin, bony woman, adjusting the microphone to her height, bringing it near her lips, articulating her lips in a precise fashion, gave voice to the words in a clear and audible way. She was the only presence on the dais; the other seven deadly sins her antitheses.

Then came the chief guest. In the fifteen-minute speech she gave, the stress was generally on the word 'figures'. 'Great damage to society will follow,' she said, 'if economists, planners, bankers, statisticians and above all, you people finger with figures. Do anything with these but never finger. This society, the great people of this great land have reposed great trust in you and you, I presume, must be aware of this trust.' The gentleman smiled abashedly.

(VIII)

Adolf. N., D.Lit., lives six months in Moscow from June to November and six months in Los Angles from December to May during which time he communicates freely with me via emails. He informed me while in Moscow, he uses his time to refresh his memories and write poems and while in Los Angles, he mails written stuff to his friends (which includes me too) for their views and then next six months in Moscow he shapes that material into self-published books. He admittedly hardly gets any comments from any of his friends and names me an exception. 'I connect in Moscow and I collect in Los Angeles' is his usual refrain.

But today he mails me this—off the routine:

Dear Dr K.K. Srivastava,

Let me hope you are OK. I have a little request. I send for *your pleasure* the Indian dance of my old friend D.T. She is PhD, senior scientific worker of the Institute of Chemical Physics, Russian Academy of Sciences, Moscow. She is a chemist but *dancing is her beloved hobby*. If you will find a couple of minutes of time, please send to her *your impression* about her dancing. It will be *big pleasure* to hear a couple of words from India.

Have a nice weekend!

Friendly,
N.

I take my own time. The words in italics befuddle me. But I oblige. Six hours later, I get another email, this time from D.T.—

Good afternoon, Mr Srivastava!
Thank you for your kind words.
I began dancing at the age of 45 to cure the sick spine. I
am, therefore, pleased to hear that someone is feeling nice
to look at my dancing.
I wish you success in good health.
D. T.

A dancer unknown despite her talents! 'You cannot know the dancer just from seeing her dance,' I thought to myself, while looking at her email.

I went to my closet this morning, after several months. How many, I don't exactly remember. Maybe after three months or even more. Usually I visit the closet every couple of days sometimes to see if the books I purchased have any value for me, sometimes just to have a look at the collections I have accumulated over four decades and sometimes to select one book I wish to read again. There are no books there I have not read at least once. A thousand odd books lie there. The thickest book in the collection is *The History of Tom Jones, A Foundling* by Henry Fielding and the thinnest—*Heart of Darkness* by Joseph Conrad. There was a diary of my uncle's from 1967 that I had kept safely and intact. Out of the 300 odd pages in the diary, he had written on three; in the rest of the diary were scribbled sketches. When he was alive, he used to shun any questions regarding the underlying meaning of those sketches but oftentimes I would find him completely engrossed with these. It was the awe on his face growing pale and fragile, as time moved, while going through the sketches that used to amuse me. It must have been a case of artistic revelation to my uncle.

(IX)

Apart from Adolf, I exchange letters with Bernard, another writer friend. Their letters convey to me what goes on in their minds sitting that far. Sharing yet another letter from a friend of mine from another country which came to me conveying his views about the country:

Dear Mr Srivastava,

Thanks for sending me [a] brief about [the] recent happenings in India and [the] modern sadhu's book. I will read in due course and get back. As of now, I am preoccupied with many more trivial tasks. Let me tell you this saint's great secret—camel milk. Then, I understand there are people infected with the incurable desire to drink urine as part of urine therapy? Please correct me if I am wrong. My memory, of late, has been failing. Then, my wife…tells me that there are many men and women there who claim to be avatars of gods and goddesses and expect an assembly of huge crowds early morning before them. Really your land is a land of marvels: each one of you is a marvel in your own capacity… I don't know your views on modern saints and the future of India and another old gentleman—whose name I am forgetting. He claims to be a crusader against corruption and at the slightest provocation sits on hunger strikes in Delhi. Why [does he] always sit on hunger strikes in only Delhi? And that too at a place called Jantar Mantar, in the heart of the city? The place of power where people abound? The place the electronic media has a powerful presence in. He would be properly taken care of. Limelight will be his. Ask him to sit where he was born. Believe me he would never [do that]. You think he is yet another saint? My wife argues with me that he is. Lookwise he appears to be. Colour. Okay. Weight. Okay. Height. Yeah. I agree. Shorter. Temperamentally, you must know better. I understand he speaks loudly and oftentimes aggressively. A great killer he is. Because of your nature, you probably do not allow yourself to talk of such things. Anyway, I truly feel India has the chance of becoming one of the most powerful and prosperous countries in business and economy. Only true leaders are needed. I think true leaders have now come: it is 2015. The people have so much passion and faith in their own land, its future, they are all so proud. This is something here in the UK we are never going to have. I am ashamed of UK for the atrocities it inflicted on India. The book that you have sent me will open my eyes up to what I knew little of. I am envious of your faiths, future, passion for being who you are in India. I can hope the new leadership brings you a whole new future, a peaceful and prosperous one. Talking with people here and listening to their views of these last few weeks, I can see how they love their country. It enthrals me. I have never witnessed my country have such passion or faith for a better future. I read some books on India and saw a documentary on India's economy and geography and must say how beautiful your country is. I was stunned and envious. One day I plan to travel there, to see its mountains, meet the people, enjoy the ambience of it all, spiritually too. Don't forget to offer me a cup or two of camel's milk. Incidentally, my wife too has liked the book. However, be aware of this old chap. My life experience, and I am nearing eighty now (and it is applicable to me too), is that old people, when left to themselves, go senile and lousy and can devastate the entire society, leave aside themselves. Please, for the sake of God, beware of these old folks apt at going on hunger strikes at the slightest possible provocation.

Best regards

S.G. Jackson, Poet and Social Analyst
UK

(X)

One day, I encounter my former boss. 'Oh, how are you? Now in Kerala, right? They have posted you there.'

'Yes sir, but how do you know this?' I politely ask. He reads my reviews in newspapers and magazines which carry my current address. I am not surprised at his usage of the word, 'they'. Why is the word 'they' so important, I don't know. The word 'we' is there. Many human relationships are founded on a tenuous connection between 'they' and 'we'. When 'they' becomes 'we' and 'we' becomes 'they', life really explores you. Exploration has a different connotation in bureaucracy. Exploration of different places; different people; different colours.

(XI)

It is as if I just heard the last dog bark and the first cock crow simultaneously, at the same time. These niceties cause curiosity in me to know about others endeavouring to ascertain the factors separating me out from the rest: partners in the ongoing scheme of things. Niceties, for some, may be charm overdone but for others it can be as cold as ice cubes. Those condemned on moral grounds search morality in lesser mortals and preach about how to make them better mortals. One example will suffice. We often hear (I have heard it at least once), some supposedly paragons of virtue, proclaiming, 'Slap so and so such loudly that next hundred years, no other can dare doing what so and so has done.' Good enough. But, does Milan Kundera not assert that one can have human rights but before that one ought to constitute himself as an individual? Unfortunately, such ladies and gentlemen reserving for themselves the divine right and virtue of identifying 'so and so' and stipulating 'such and such punishment' as an eye-opener for posterity, fail to ask a simple question to themselves. Have these purveyors of righteous wisdom constituted, organized and arranged themselves in a way so as to acquire such a divine virtue and right? This is a very important lesson I have learnt in the arena of social niceties. 'Holier than thou' is a faith religiously followed there.

What I miss here, I get from friends like Jackson and Adolf.

The compensation is not only adequate but also varied. Adolf asking me to see the dance of her lady friend who suffers from a sick spine, and expecting me to write to her a few words about my impressions of her dance, represents to me a lofty form of emotional equilibrium a writer of repute like Adolf can exhibit towards his dancer friend. Likewise, Jackson, far away from here, expressing his belief in India of today and reposing his faith in the present efforts for the future good of society is an example to cherish. Jackson maintains an objective distance and those who do that can assess truth and express that truth undauntedly, something I really miss while indulging in social niceties here.

CHAPTER **11**

Women of Literature and Women in Literature

(I)

One would think, getting confronted directly with the confessional intensity of works of a female writer is like the icing on the cakes. It is alluring to think of such a scenario where two jobs need to be performed by the one who confronts such a writer—maintaining a distance from and an intimacy with the female writer. It helps in having what is alive as a leftover at the end. One is at one with the fluttering and flickering of feathers. For me it was to happen in a coffee house in Lucknow, in May 2017.

∫

Conversation with a female author is the best way to understand what propels her to write what she writes. I invited Ms B for that purpose and she turned up at ten past six. A delay of ten minutes seemed immaterial. She preferred orange juice and said an emphatic 'no' when the waiter asked how many sugar cubes she would like to take in the juice. After a while, she looked at me sparingly and uttered, 'Okay.'

'What of tragic events in your novels? I quipped.

'Absurd, absurd. No, I don't think so. You bring your characters alive in your books. Icon is the greatest power of my works,' she grumbled; stress was on 'my'.

'You find every bit in your unconscious. There are characters who are reading certain lines the way you think they should read. I think if they can do it, why can't I. That is how literature does things. It changes sensibilities; it changes the way I write.' She again looked into my eyes for roughly thirty seconds and as I was trying to read into hers, I realized that the battle was already lost. I got nothing there.

'And depicting adversities,' I said.

She paused inadvertently and continued, 'My refuge has been irony and satire. You can deal with satire but it is very difficult to deal with irony.' The discussion was taking a discreet turn. 'Nothing is related to irony. Anything in literature can be trivialized but not irony. The writer is always at a distance. I say words are like tirade and through this tirade you look at yourself.'

'Cynicism also...' I tried to butt in but she was with herself, the pace she determined, 'I don't think I have totally escaped cynicism. I do believe you are sceptical about anything. You also realize you hit rock-bottom, then you again come out.' She looked at her wristwatch. 'You manage to survive—there is a turn about it. Everything changes—that is the only truth about my writing. You believe that people are sceptical when they see the outer world and they behave accordingly.'

'But critics maintain your novels beguile,' another cryptic intervention.

'Look, gentleman,' she looked grim and serious, 'your disillusionment with the world, your disillusionment about the world, your disillusions about yourself—all these represent true disillusionment. It is a simple model. Am I responsible for it? Yes, I am. Once you accept it, you are a good commentator. It is this participation in whatever is happening around you that does not make me cynical. I am sceptical, you know.'

'You seem to be going somewhere…the society, female writers, language, relevance,' I buttonholed.

'Maybe but I don't believe in changing any structure, any values attached. I also say that like the birth of a person, writing has also its birth. There are both positives and negatives, I mean sensations: society dictates these sensitivities, these sensations, but I feel the need for personal censorship. I believe there is a great difference between men and women, in their sensibilities, perceptions, but historically women have been trained to differ. It is not a conscientious world—in power both are the same. Being very critical of each other, I mean: man-woman relationships, perhaps, founded my creativity and thinking. Feminism means what? A simulation. Each woman is different from the rest—no clear demarcation—mother-housewife, working woman-housewife. Each one different from the other. They don't aspire to be the same thing. A woman is compassionate. Feminism creates its own world which is really bad and counterproductive. I want to work not because you want me to do it but it is my choice. If you can't choose, you are insulating. I have seen many successful women bemoaning their having no children when they cross 50. Feminism is not ultimate freedom. Feminism has limitations. Those who believe in it must believe in its limitations.'

'Yeah, you asked me about, what was that—,' she was no longer curious.

'Language,' I said.

'Language is not addition of new words—it is your language. If you can't play with language, something goes. Something is amiss. Now we are in a stage where language is lost. It is a thing of beauty. That beauty is lost. It adds beauty to your content. Experimental path. It takes characters from life. And then believe in them. Literature is not business. If it is at all business, it is a bad business,' she averred.

'When I write,' she continued, 'I deal with both dreams and realities. I find them both stark. My husband once told me plainly that I must consult a psychiatrist. A psychiatrist is a false physician. The average shaman has more validity. Maybe my dreams, my realities are not destitute, maybe they are just in hiding, awaiting discovery. Then readers become relevant; they act as psychiatrists,' she was more sober a little while back. 'And as far as individuality in writings is concerned, I would remind you that writers, like everybody else, do not live or learn in vacuum. They are influenced by who and what they read. To tell a modern writer that I hear echoes of Brecht or Rilke in his writings isn't meant at all to denigrate his work. Rather it's a compliment. He might not have had Brecht or Rilke in mind when he wrote his lines. He might not have even heard of these names as is the case with the majority of bestselling writers of modern times. So be it. A writer must always wrestle with various influences. He should pull away but he always takes something of the earlier influence with him. So, a writer's individuality is often determined by those who came before him. That's just how it is. I hope every writer I've read has left his mark in his own writing, in some way, however small it might be. By the way that's not plagiarism; it's an acknowledgment of something publishers don't understand.'

'And now middlemen dubbed as literary agents?' I was keen to see her reaction to my observation.

∽

'I must tell you, these bloody book awards, publishers who have names, they never attract me. Once they invited me as an observer:

to look after the fairness with which business was being conducted. My job was only to observe and then report, not to be involved in the process of selection; my job was to only ensure fairness. And you know what I witnessed there? A round table. Seven indifferent people like corpses (young editors of a prestigious publishing house meant for reading manuscripts) sitting in the room to deliberate upon what makes a book flourish i.e., who is the best among the best shortlisted few to get the chance to be published—the criteria: "Are only thoughts random, or also the characters. Is there scope for the different characters or thoughts to make a reappearance under different moods, or circumstances?"

The crux of criteria: Light fiction telling a great story.

> First indifferent man says, "I think the writer must write like a painter of modern art."
> Second indifferent man says, "Each stroke of the brush is random, seemingly."
> Third indifferent man says, "And the reader can draw a different perspective."
> Fourth indifferent man says, "Depending on his state of mind."
> Fifth indifferent man says, "The meaning of the lines and quotes might be related to someone else's state of mind."
> Sixth indifferent man says, "But the reader can draw a different inference."
> Seventh indifferent man says, "Depending on the writer's state of mind."

> Seven corpses of indifferent people remained indecisive and spent the rest of the day staring at each other indifferently, evoking no sense of ennui. Stupid language imprisons itself. Decision not deferred. All manuscripts rejected. Light fiction telling a great story. Search on.'

'So impulsive, you may agree,' the woman said. 'That was the first and perhaps the last time I was invited. Being fair is a great vice.'

'And of rating of poetry books and awards?' Where else would I get an opportunity to elicit opinion on such issues and that too from such a well-known female author? So, I asked her.

Ms B did not mind answering, 'I have written more than twelve poetry collections though not yet sure if I may be placed in the league of renowned poets. My profile describes me neither as an award-winning poet nor were my books included in the yearly selection of top ten poets during say 2016. One such selection was of twenty poetry books for the year 2016 in a 'prestigious magazine' owned by a business family. The selection was by a lady poet of 25 who the editor described as 'a renowned poet'. She kept my book out as expected and ranked first and second of those who by virtue of their sheer ignorance happen to be heading a jury ready to pronounce their ultimate wisdom in terms of pronouncing literary awards for poetry for 2015. Award announced—the 25-year-old, tall, dusky lady, the hottest toast of literati, stole it. The citation described her as an example of the finest poetry juggling with reality representing a whiff of dawn breeze. Methinks the 75-year-old man, himself a poet adjudging her as winner, must be suffering from senility of uncontrollable romantic passions. Literature dies the moment senile old men start assessing young poetess's works.

Later in early dinner party hosted by the young winner, where I was also invited, her obsession with words like "post-colonial", "Derrida" and "magical realism" was remarkable. She really admired people who are virtually twenty-four hours a day on social sites, busy smiling, laughing, praising each other, liking, sharing, putting incisive comments and still producing book after book. When do they write? Really unbelievable.

Only time she did not talk was when she sipped wine.

The 75-year-old poet judge hardly able to stand, was seen clapping.'

(II)

Aaj Savere (This morning)—a national Doordarshan programme features conversation with writers. The invitation from them is for me for a conversation with a female anchor on a book of poetry. Silence is to be dissected.

The major issue the interviewer raised is still agitating my mind. The more I am trying to keep that issue at bay, the more I feel vexed.

'Why do you write such long poems and for whom? Don't you know people have no time for poetry? Long poems are stillborn poems.' I could not tackle the question then but these were the remains of what she told me. Remains still lingering with me and not leaving me. Perhaps because I relish long poems as they substitute for stories or tales but with nature not clear. Deadness of long poems? Dead things never give me a cosy feeling. Dead things are like monolithic structures—sucking, sucking and always sucking.

'Muktibodh—the Hindi poet—died in misery, of brain fever. Well known but not affluent poets of Hindi were with him when he died in impoverished conditions. He left behind material that would get him fame—slow but steady—that would make him a *kaaljayi kavi*, a poet who is beyond time. Fortunate writers are those who live after their death and leave a lot of unpublished material. Long back, Kafka wanted the material he left behind not to be published but to be burnt after his death—a desire Jorge Luis Borges seriously questioned. "Why did Kafka not burn his manuscripts himself?" Borges posed this question. A very genuine question. A very serious question. Hats off to

Borges. Why did others not feel the way Borges felt? Who will answer this? Our Muktibodh was more pragmatic; wisdom was with him, foresightedness was his forte. He knew the capacity of contemporary or the subsequent generation of writers to question even the least ingenuous works. He took no chances; he left the fate of his unpublished material in hands he never bothered to think of. He had no posthumous desires.'

The only book Muktibodh could see in his lifetime is *Ek Sahityik ki Diary* (Diary of a Litterateur), a thin book running into 120 pages by Muktibodh which lay on my table. I rearranged the books—something I had a desire to do once every three months. Last night, this book seemed to have been left out on the table or perhaps had fallen on the ground, and the maid, while sweeping the room early morning, on noticing it, had kept it back on the table. Anything displaced in that room from its usual place found its ultimate destination—the table—courtesy the maid.

Lo and behold. Here is a favourite author of mine ready to hand over all the answers the interviewer was seeking. Look carefully at the title: 'The End of a Long Poem'. Muktibodh, as I know him through his writings—his very long poems—is a poet groping in extreme darkness and spotting darkness even under a scorching sun. But first see the example he gave towards the end of the narration. I am using the word 'narration' deliberately as his Diary is chaptered but sequenced with no dates or months. For the writer of 'The End of a Long Poem' the end was of utmost importance. Please read that and draw your conclusions.

Huge, well spread out, awe-inspiring boundaries. A gigantic bungalow—very old, dilapidated, mysterious and empty. Entry is prohibited. A man enters there and meets another man: seemingly a spy, and yet another man, a complete lunatic. Underneath the ground the bungalow had staircases spread out to different countries, to the clock tower of the city and also to the zenith of the human brain. Everyone in that bungalow had made adjustments and in the process had crumbled down, their hearts ruptured—the soul of the bungalow was dead. The bungalow seemed to be possessed by monkey-rule, a negativity in full display. The soul was dead and people mired into silence for they had made adjustments, profiting from the adjustments, not willing to part with the profits out of adjustments. Muktibodh had communist leanings.

Muktibodh, as he tells us, is dealing with an allegory which gives a poem a longish form. Telling either the realities of present society or a play where characters present themselves in real forms to portray life's realities. Leave aside music, a poem for him is the most abstract art form: experimenting with ideas, symbols or metaphors with all the drama inside the poem representing nothing but dynamics of symbols or metaphors. A long poem stretches out to various, innumerable roots of the human psyche and brain.

He treats long poems as long plays human beings take part in—each play portraying a wounded, wrecked and offended interplay of characters unable to move out of the ordinariness of life foisted upon them. In this long journey, Muktibodh stresses the role of dead sensibilities in making out of a long poem. It's here that humanness surrenders itself to the social desire towards earning profit, the essential crisis occurring as a result of an indecisive human nature causing poets to pen long poems. Each poet writing long poems has his moments of warmth but the dark and deep moments from where he has emerged, the poet never forgets.

(III)

Professor Perry, an American poet, thanked me for my offer to send him my book of poems. He wanted me to recall that the final issue of a reputed journal (not proper to mention its name for fear of copyright violations) contained an essay by him which indicated (perhaps too obliquely) that he was not a good judge of Indian poetry in English, because the underlying culture and aesthetic was not one he had been able to absorb (knowing no other Indian language besides English). Then he asked me to look into his essay in another esteemed journal wherein he did not apologize for that limitation, but he had since come to feel and decide firmly that he should cease to comment on poetry from India altogether. India and poetry—unthinkable!

He found my offer of sending my book to him quite flattering but was stubborn that he would not comment on it, and probably would not read more than a snippet from it.

Professor Perry argued a lot before agreeing with India's enormously diverse poetry and poetic traditions but added, 'No Indian poet is the end of Indian poetry.' He expected me to understand his position as an American who had tried for many years but still did not fully engage with the Indian poetic traditions and their underlying aesthetic value systems. All this while he was very blunt; he could make out that my failure to understand him was either because despite asking for it, I did not really care about what he thought or that I was myself stuck in a peculiar position in some mental area perhaps of imagination and intellect that he himself could not possibly understand. To cure this, it was his prescription, that I read with some care the last essay he wrote for the final issue of that literary journal once more—without letting my prejudices and jealousies overcome my search for meaning. If I then got a better sense of his position as laboriously laid out there, he would appreciate an acknowledgement of my errors in continuing to badger him about my or any other Indian poetry. He hoped for clarity and compassion. 'One day God will give you Indian writers wisdom,' were Professor Perry's words to me. He meant business.

But Professor Perry was keen to understand the link between

the title of my third poetry collection—*Shadows of the Real*—and the sixty-seven poems making that title. So there was an unwanted task before me. The soul is a self-thinker. Soul and existence are like two individual entities. The title is expressive, yet subtle. Something that is transfixed, making one feel motionless, making one sense the intensity of this title. It is, as if something of truth in the shadows of my mind is now becoming vague, weakening... Shadows of the past or the present. Does a blissful state greet me? I feel as if my thoughts have been deeply moved by loss of love and faith. Something one thinks precious has now become a disappointment. Questioning thoughts that were truth, once upon a time, but are now fading into the distance. In a spiritual sense, it seems final. It makes one's mind sad after reading the title for some reason, but it has an inner spirituality; it is like the inner-self attempting to repel its own desires and impulses, images of memories or images of present being. There are shadows—an inexorably obnoxious contrivance. But to whom am I to explain it? Who can convince a man of letters from abroad?

I sent the interview with a Maltese poet by email for his consideration. Professor Perry told me he would read it when he had the time to do so; he was delighted to receive it but when he would read it, nobody knew. He was busy with writing articles and submissions but was very trustworthy. Once he promised to read something, he would keep his promise but then when? A big question. None ought to hazard any guess. That was the irresistible beauty of Professor Perry's mind to me given his Hindu philosophy of life. He hoped the interview would merit consideration for publication. He claimed to be a serious person, and because the magazine he was associated with was also international, he was always busy. It came out four times a year. He would give time till the middle of next month and then would expect me to enquire. He did not like to be pushed. I was glad Professor Perry had asked me to familiarize myself with some of the poets on his list. Familiarizing oneself with poets who often had work submitted to his journal always helped.

But Professor Perry believed that there are no writers in India, only bloggers. Indians make good bloggers. 'India's bestselling writers produce lewd and pale literature,' he was clear in his conclusion.

(IV)

Women in literature: Pablo Neruda versus D.H. Lawrence. Beginning has been a great riddle. Is it provisional? Is it not? It is the way one begins. Looking at things around. There are so many things around me. Oftentimes, one wonders at things desired and not found, the way there are things undesired but in your lap like her complaint which was unusual. Carla D's lips had not been kissed for years: thirteen years, to be precise. Are you sure? Are you sure she told you this? That her lips had not been kissed for thirteen years? Yes. She seemed genuine. Was it a complaint? Against whom? Must be one she expected to plant a kiss on her lips.

∽

Of the fairer sex it is often arguably debated that its members possess lethal capabilities to take any man by utter surprise. Any time. Jaipur. I was heading a training institute. This time, a young girl, whose name I have forgotten, came at four that afternoon, a frosty one. There wasn't much work in training institutes, you know. 'Side-postings.' Are you hearing me? Why don't you confess that lady has just stopped laughing? Laugh on the sly. A flash of thought overpowers me. You say something. You speak out your views. The lady was young, her date of birth was 13 July 1980, fair but short, maybe five feet or slightly lesser. She held my book in her hand. 'Sit down please,' I said. She sat down.

'Name please.' She named herself. She—'I admire your intellectual capabilities.'

I—'Hmm. You have come to tell me this.'

She—'I got this book from the library and read it and enjoyed it.'

I—'Like to have tea?'

Silence. I persist with my query, she, with her silence. One silence won over the other. Tea is served; she appears quite eager, I wishful. Sipping hot tea had its own pleasure. She licked her lips. Twice. My eyes enjoyed that. She sat silently.

She—'I love your poem "Immutabilities"; unique imagery, bathroom scene.'

I—'Okay.' All along she had been anything but at rest.

'Why don't you write something on shadows? It interests me,' she asks as I try to look into her eyes; two black pupils meet mine momentarily and then she lowers her eyelids. I get her.

Aftermath—Ezra Pound's lines:

> Bah! I have sung women in three cities
> But it is all the same...

∽

Jaipur. I used to sit under the big mango tree for two hours or little less. This tree was one of the many surrounding the bungalow I had been given as part of the facilities accorded to one in charge of heading the institute.

It was a very big house with five big bedrooms, a drawing-cum-dining room equipped to accommodate fifty guests at a time, huge lawns with more than thirty trees, big and small, and well-trimmed grass that I used to walk on early morning sipping my first cup of tea. By the time I came to that bungalow, my grip over my solitude was so tightly shaped that it was virtually hermetic and during four years of my stay there, no one excepting my wife, two sons, and myself, visited it.

It was a place my fullness met its drabness; it was a place I was most comfortable in. Lots of ideas took root in that environment, words came effortlessly.

I recall the dining table in that house. Although suitable for eight people surrounded as it was with eight chairs, it would, at a time, be occupied by either only me or my wife. My wife and my good self never dined together; she said she was extremely uncomfortable in my company at the dining table though I took extreme care to ensure this complaint did not continue and persist afterwards in bed.

I like Neruda for his instantaneous love with his lines:

> They say terrible things
> about a man and a woman
> who, after much milling about,
> all sorts of compunction,
> do something unique—
> they both lie with each other in one bed.

Neruda seemed to be among one of the many 'poor fellows'.

∫

D.H. Lawrence's concerns about women run thus:

> The feelings, I don't have I don't have,
> The feelings I don't have, I won't say I have,
> The feelings you say you have, you don't have,
> The feelings you would like us both to have, we neither
> of us have.
> The feelings people ought to have, they never have…

> If people say they've got feelings, you may be pretty sure
> they have not got them.
> So if you want either of us to feel anything at all
> you'd better abandon all idea of feelings altogether.

I told Professor Yadav, 'Sir, Lawrence must have been let down very much.' Professor Yadav responded, 'My mother, like yours, was a woman of wisdom. My mother, like yours, used to caution my father of other women's "triyacharitra" which even the Trinity of Gods—Brahma, Vishnu and Mahesh cannot tackle and predict. I respect Lawrence who must have been a victim of "triyacharitra" of the women closest to him. Lawrence looked at women as a bundle of fully-exhausted possibilities. There is nothing more to explore; Lawrence might have explored everything before reaching this apocalyptic situation. He sacrificed the sanctity of women. And that too with a sense of responsibility.

And look KK, sometimes I pity you and sometimes I pity myself for you being my student. You have wasted my time in making me think and discussing about this fellow—Lawrence. The chap measures man-woman relationships only in terms of "have" or "don't have".

Professor Yadav's departing words made me cautious of his anger. I was sanguine he meant it. Though I feel happy to have paid generous homages to a few of my friends for their efforts to remove obscurity through their opinions, I wish my uncle could be alive to give me a holistic picture of what I gained and what I lost.

CHAPTER 12

A Half-made Place and Its People

I was being restless with no alternative available and open; I latched on to madam Mahavipida Devi's words—vividly transparent, though she lacked complete transparency in her public dealings. 'You don't meet the parameters for placement in any of the four posh places you have requested. Have you understood?'

Professor Yadav, on hearing that this was what had happened to me, counselled, 'Boss, the lady gave you an opportunity to ruminate and write about a place where those meeting the parameters for placement in posh places are never or rarely posted. KK, convert bad events into opportunities and challenges into pieces of writing. Don't conceal pain which is personal but caused by malodorous persons like that lady.' He could not incite me much for bad memories like the conversation with the lady really marred my gusto, but he persisted, 'KK, you have been critical of your birthplace, but tell me, of all the places you have seen, why don't you select one you think was not a desirable place; a half-made society, but abounding with lousy people? Even without participating in sad remembrances, as a detached witness, you can narrate. You have the skills.'

I know it wouldn't be a comforting experience. Still I must attempt it, for not attempting to write about a memory that causes pain is akin to pardoning the culprits causing that pain, and such writers must, then, be doomed to suffer in true Hindu tradition.

∫

November 2004.

As the flight was readying to land at Zuddupur, I saw dense clouds and could sense the wind, well, almost. Twice the plane zoomed up as landing was difficult due to very poor visibility. Late by an hour, it finally landed to the relief of the passengers. 'The outside temperature is 26 degree celcius and it has been raining. Please take with you all your belongings like spectacles, books, mobiles, etc. We thank you again for flying with us and hope you will fly with us again.' The announcement by the air hostess ended. I guessed it was the same air hostess who had served us snacks and tea. I looked at her long fingers that rapidly moved while serving plates mechanically as if no emotions were involved in the task. While many passengers ogled at her, she hardly noticed them; it felt as if she was moving among dead people sitting. 'Their training is such. They are trained to ignore ogling eyes. They are trained to accept it as a price for their being in this job,' a colleague of mine had told me once while he was travelling with me.

Outside, it was a welcome change as I felt the fresh, cool air brushing past me. It was a small airport and from the staircase to the entrance, I had to cover a distance of about 50 meters. One had to walk as no transport was provided to the passengers.

∫

I wanted to hire a taxi. I was to stay there for a couple of months and since I intended to travel in and around that place, I wanted a taxi which could be with me for the two months I would be there saving me the bother of locating different taxis on different days. I saw several kinds of vehicles outside. Some were white ambassadors with red and yellow beacon lights meant for politicians and bureaucrats. With those lights on, ordinary people are made to realize that only those dignitaries whose designations are displayed on the cars are travelling by the car. If some of the bureaucrats are even more important, then a pilot vehicle usually precedes their cars with a blazing and noisy siren alerting people constantly of the bureaucrat's arrival. There are black ambassadors too with the same paraphernalia. These are used by officers from the army.

Then there were private cars and autos. Autos can carry two passengers in the back seat and if one is thin, then three. Though no one is allowed to sit on the drivers' sides, drivers allow one person to sit beside them provided, just before any traffic signal (where cops stand), the passenger gets down, cross the traffic by foot and reoccupy his seat in the same auto which waits for him after having crossed the traffic signal. This allows being not caught by the cops.

The auto I hired had a big 'Om' sign inscribed on its front just below the glass with the message 'God helps all who help others'. On the back, was written *'Buri nazarwale, tera muha kala'* (Evil-eyed ones, let you face turn black.) The auto driver had a thin physique, was swarthy in colour and was smoking a bidi. I asked him, 'Why have you put these inscriptions?' Very unwillingly, and only on my repeating the question, he said to me, 'I don't own this auto. It belongs to my uncle. He has another part-time job. He cannot keep the auto idle; I am his nephew and I drive it. He charges me 50 per cent of what I earn. As the inscriptions were already there, I can't reveal the correct motive behind it, but I can hazard a guess. Our religion teaches us to wish others well, so the message in the front. As this is a small place with limited traffic and virtually no fresh avenues of employment, there is fierce competition among auto owners to attract passengers. At times, other auto owners wish others ill to keep business to themselves; hence the message on the back of the auto is a warning to such persons.'

'Your earnings per day?' I asked as I felt my temptation rise. He was interesting to interact with. The auto driver kept mum. 'On an average?' I persisted.

'Not fixed. It varies from five to fifty rupees but I have not earned in three figures on any single day though I have been running an auto since the last two years. I don't run it on Sundays.'

'Sundays for rest,' I quipped. He fell into silence again. This time I chose not to ask him again. After a while his answer surfaced, 'Sundays are for haircut.'

'You go for a haircut every Sunday?' My question seemed to have no effect on him. He kept controlling the auto without much concern for passers-by.

'No, I work as an assistant in a hair salon and Sunday being a holiday, provides a good number of persons for haircuts.'

'How much do you get there?'

'Fifty, it is fixed.'

I reached the destination. My sojourn with him was over.

Taking an average of forty rupees per day from driving an auto multiplied by twenty-six and fifty every Sunday and dividing that by four gave the driver a monthly income of about Rs 1240 to 1300; about forty rupees a day. Finding it difficult to locate taxies on the roads, I decided to continue with the same auto-rickshaw if he agreed. He agreed on a fixed sum of Rs 60 per day with cost of petrol to be given separately. Out on the road one day, I could see heavy traffic from a distance at the crossroad approximately hundred metres away, while a lowly paid policeman with a big belly was trying to helplessly regulate the traffic. After a while he gave up and stood in a corner. As it would take some time to proceed on that road anyway, I got down to seeing for myself what had gone wrong. The tolerance was remarkable. Nobody seemed to mind the chaos on the road. People were as if deafened, tolerating all of it with the equanimity of a hermit.

Near the crossroad, some festive occasion was being celebrated and roughly fifty people from different age groups formed a crowd. Through a loudspeaker, a lewd song in Bhojpuri (an Indo-Aryan language spoken in some parts of North India) was in the air: '*Aarahile, Chaprahile, Calcutta hile la, jab lachake tu har kamaria*', in honour of a lady dancer with the task of entertaining an excitable crowd. (Aara, Chapra and Calcutta—the three districts from Bihar and West Bengal.) I attempt a rough translation—

'Aara shakes,
Chapra shakes,
Calcutta shakes,
When a woman's
Waist wriggles.'

Powerful imagination to display woman power, I thought. The song would stop every few seconds for announcements made by a man with a grating voice. At one point, he declared that a famous Bhojpuri singer had already started from a neighbouring district and requested that the crowd gather at night to hear him. Announcement over, the song resumed to suit a set pattern. Everyone was thrilled.

A few yards away, there was another cluster of people, apparently watching something interesting. The small crowd consisted of males from different age groups: students, educated people, rustics and children. Some of them were laughing hard alongside clapping happily at something. Upon reaching closer, I was struck by the sight. What the people had been staring at was a gigantic dog mating a thin bitch, the latter yelling from time to time. This bare demonstration of animal instinct provided adequate stimuli to the avid viewers. I wondered if we require any sex education in such places. I often wonder how these events, perfectly natural for the dogs, arrest the attention of people so completely. It does not arouse, in any onlooker, a sense of shame in the sheer unabashed fun out of the voyeuristic activity they indulge in. Instead, they transfer this very gaze onto other subjects, possible prey, to their sexual instincts. They succumb to their animal instinct but not quite respectfully.

It had turned cloudy and I was in a hurry. The guest house where I was going to put up in was still five kilometres away.

While on my way further, I saw at a distance, five to six men and women bent as if searching for something. The women appeared thin and emaciated. When I moved closer to find out what they were up to, I realized that they were trying to draw the maximum water possible from whatever water was pouring out of a pipe hardly six inches above the ground. There was no tap to regulate the flow.

The women had with them five to six plastic containers which seemed to have been used for storing either oil or ghee by its former owners who had eventually discarded them. The containers had once been a distinct green or yellow but were now faded. These women would have collected the containers from garbage heaps. Like nothing goes waste in a jungle and every bit of consumable thing is consumed, here, in human societies too, what is wasted by one fulfils another's desire. We take care of each other.

The women took turns to try and direct the flow of water towards these containers with much difficulty. Suddenly, I saw a boy of six or seven years, totally naked, come running down from nowhere in a great haste. He sat down four to five feet away from where the tap water was being lifted, to defecate. This caused no annoyance to anyone on the spot. A little later, after he had finished, one of the women, perhaps the boy's mother, poured water from her container on to the boy's back cleaning it with her foot. Soon after, the woman, without throwing the leftover water she had used to clean her son, filled the same again for her daily chores. I felt sickened by what paucity can make one do. But we are tolerant, since we see this almost every day; hence we are sensitive to neither irritation nor gloom for long.

My discomfiture, however, was on the rise. The evening was getting cooler; darkness was falling. I reached the guest house around 8 in the evening and went to bed. I was in need of sleep. Badly.

∼

I was supposed to take the train from station X but I was prevailed upon by Bhilu Bhai, the auto driver, to board it from Y, another station located at a distance of four kilometres from station X. The platform was relatively clean with fifteen to twenty passengers around. The train was yet to be brought to the platform and the man to attend to queries from the passengers was not present on the enquiry counter, nor was there anyone to make any enquiries. To idle away the time, accompanied with Bhilu Bhai who did show an uncalled-for courtesy in accompanying me to the platform to help me board the train, I decided to roam around the small railway platform.

There were three benches—coloured yellow and black with black stripes—for passengers to sit. Two of the benches were occupied by two men, fairly young, ageing perhaps thirty to thirty-five, and one of them was actually snoring loudly causing disturbance in an otherwise very quiet atmosphere. It was comical to witness a rhythmic rise and fall of his thick belly and similarly a rhythmic jerk in his lower portion with the tail-end of every snore. The third bench was occupied with three briefcases indicating the presence of their owner somewhere close by.

Bhilu Bhai wanted me to go along with him to a restaurant located at platform number 1, though I was not able to take note of its presence. Around ten feet away, it was displayed: 'Pundit ji ka Dukaan' (Punditji's shop). On entering the shop, the first thing I was keen to do was have a cup of coffee. However, the Nescafe coffee machine was out of order!

'Since when?' I asked.

The boy did not bother to take note of the question and asked, 'Will you take tea as only tea can be supplied now?'

'Has the coffee machine been out of order for a long time?' I asked again wondering if it was not running due to lack of electricity.

'No, sahib, as we do not get anyone asking for coffee, we got a damaged machine fixed on the very first day the hotel was opened. We never use it. *Iski bhi... saaley ki kismet fati hai.*' (This bastard's fate is also ruined.)

'How much time will you take to prepare tea?'

'No time. Tea is already ready. I will reboil it immediately.' The boy bowed and lifted the kettle which appeared to be containing some liquid and put it on the stove that already was being used to boil potatoes. After boiling it for two minutes, he picked up a half-strained cup and poured the hot brown liquid into it.

I heard a sound. The train was about to arrive on the tracks. I was soliloquising.

Santosh Danny, a local businessman into IT, the buck-toothed man, had a strange past.

He had been having, as he claimed, bizarre experiences during the last twenty-eight years which he planned to put together in a book and he had been at it for quite some time now. Even before the world could come to know about it all though, I was granted access to some of his strange experiences, of course because I requested it.

About to be three years old, Danny was made to adopt Christianity and he eventually became a true and ardent supporter of religious conversions. Now fifty-four, he had a graphic memory of what had exactly occurred around that time. Forcing him to alter his religion. He did not care whether his memories were believed or not. One day, I was seated in his chambers and he began,

'I was, KK, born of parents none of whom could boast of either the riches that make life comfortable or the beauties that shake passers-by. My father was as lean and lanky as I am though less swarthy, and my mother, five times as waxy as my father and half his size. They did not make an ideal couple, not at least physically. The one characteristic both of them shared in great abundance was the darkness in the colour of their skin and yellowish teeth. You might not agree because you, as I understand, have seen neither misery nor misfortune. Let me tell you, my parents like many more poor people on earth, might have been niggardly in all respects but when it came to distributive justice of their genes, they liberally passed them on in more or less equal proportion to their fourteen children. I know you may ask me how I make this statement.' Danny paused for a while, looking at me, his glance more questioning than revealing. He now looked at the monitor of his computer, using the mouse to locate something. After five minutes his right arm moved, picked up the cheroot from the ashtray and took a drag on it. A deep one. 'No mails. So far. The chap must have forgotten. Always busy with her: the P.S.' Danny, expecting a return mail reply about supplies for his business from his partner, looked tired, anguish making his dark face darker. 'I will take another five minutes. Waiting for an important message. Okay, see this photograph.' He pulled the drawer of his table and took out a framed photograph. I took it.

The photograph reminded me of things antique, shorn off and abhorring. Around four by three inches, black and white, anyone could guess how old it must be. For me too, hazarding a guess was the only option. The white portions of the photograph had faded significantly but the main characters forming the central part of the photo were intact. I counted; they were fourteen.

One old man, an old woman, nine boys, some of whom were sufficiently old enough to be called boys, and three girls. A little girl, perhaps three years old, was in the woman's lap. I guessed the woman to be the mother. Sometimes you are with someone whose mere presence is difficult to miss. The man exuded no confidence in the photograph. He distinguished himself only by virtue of his broad smile which exposed his teeth spectacularly well in the photograph.

'You will no doubt, question, at least, to begin with, my name. What is in the name? Don't you remember this? Yes, my name was not Danny then, I mean when I was named just after I was born. My parents had an uncanny ability to name their children assigning strange names to all of them: names that signalled strange meanings. Look at these names. Dukhiya (sadness), Bhikhari (beggar), Narakia (hellish), Shokiya (happiness), Swargia (heavenly), Mootana (pissing), Dukhharna (sucker of sadness), etc. Our circumstances were full of woe and misery, suffocation and poverty. My parents could possibly think of no names excepting the ones that resembled these circumstances. Circumstances make leaders. Sometimes misdirected leaders too; in fact, it is always the latter that is more in number. My name was also not Danny but Deen. Deen, you know, implies a poor, helpless person. Anyone looking at me and my siblings in the photograph, that you are holding, cannot find fault with the logic of my parents naming their children so pathetically. Yes, with me came my name. Deen, the poor, the helpless. I was made to realize that names emanate from the circumstances one is born into and is reared up amidst. How lucky are the animals? They don't need names.'

Santosh Danny was sounding like a super cool customer. He was in a tearing hurry to leave: he was to attend a conversion camp.

I found Santosh Danny's bizarre experience linked with naming children after circumstances not a new experience for me. There are so many half-made places in India and elsewhere and with unabated conversions, no dearth of people like Santosh Danny.

On hearing my brave experiences in such a place, Professor Yadav said quite lightly, 'You must be a lucky man to have seen so many places. I understand your wife also hails from a small place. Sometimes one must get opportunities to see and interact with half-made places and their inhabitants. These tell you of life and you may even get a partner while on that journey: wife or a husband. You cannot confine yourself to two or three places and expect to have a life partner.' I was doubly convinced with Professor Yadav's worldly wisdom. The train arrived and I was on my way to Chandigarh.

CHAPTER 13

Of Social Media

Reality is a dream. By the time you realize it, half of your life has been lived and you are not sure if the half left over, belongs to you at all. Quirks of your own and those of your acquaintances are what you deal with and imaginative amplification further on is left to social media. Social media fills the gap: it has really revolutionized connections, communications, dreams and reaches; it has helped people in having a cosmos of impressions some of which can be deceptive too. Social media, the most endearing phenomenon of modern times, gives me inter alia, two things: strange faces and strange names. A perfect place to look at without any joy, any emotions whatsoever and always returning from it more confused than ever. It clubs one and all with alienation asymmetrically spread out. It introduces one to the artificial world where real, discontented people live their lives satisfactorily. Social media is where most are like damn mascots, meaningless persons expecting serious conversation about the rubbish they write. I hate it. It is impossible to be faithful on social media. There are all kinds of love out there and hearts sway this way and that. Social media is a charade, it does not contain true beings. It's like a fairy tale. Ubiquitous surfaces hide expressions of things platonic. Unnatural relationships are garbed in romantic gestures.

༶

I saw this in my inbox the other day: 'I saw your profile on internet and I would like to know you—I can send some hot pictures of mine if you want. I am online right now so you can contact me… and I will send you pictures in 5 minutes. Kisses… Sheena.'

I continued thinking of Sheena's kisses, Sheena's hot pictures…

'Where are you lost?' my watchful wife quips. I tell her of Sheena's kisses and hot pictures.

'Some women can only think of and see things that are lewd. Block her or throw away the PC,' her cold voice chafes.

Ms Lehanga changed her profile picture. I guess it was due to my mailing her my views of her. I mailed her mine. She obliged. I got the meaning of what she said or even what she didn't overtly. I understood her perfectly. And perhaps she too. Funny, how life bestows us with the gift to connect with another soul, make connections that are more heartfelt than those that involve touch. She wrote: 'You are my type of person: respectful, generous, kind, loving in a silent way, intelligent, passionate about writing, a really good soul, dominant in a sense; everything about you is just so wonderful. What do you think of this photo of mine? Tell me what you feel. Three photos: first, when I was 32; second, 38 and last, 48. Now tell me which one you like the most and why. Which one do you feel at ease with?'

A year has gone by. I am unable to decide whether to respond to Ms Lehanga or not. God knows when the wisdom to decide will dawn on me.

༶

Social media provides a great opportunity for experiments. It is all about experiments. I stand convinced.

Ms Lehanga deleted and blocked Bulu, as he might try to come back. She deleted English Poet James Pacs and Fluid Cooks too, as she found and told me what these creeps were like. She deleted this man called Gany, she did not trust him. She also deleted a man that came yesterday: another poet from Canada. She was saddened these men did not take her seriously as a person. And James Pacs had truly made her feel sick. Unbelievable. She deleted Rony Firanga too, for she found him to be a disgusting specimen of a human being. 'He has a mouth like a sewer and his manners are disgraceful, so he has to go too.'

'I am harsh or do you think I was overreacting?' she requests for my reaction. On my failing to respond, this is what creeps in from Ms Lehanga: 'Some of those men and women, my goodness. They still send requests. I add, then delete. So many ridiculous messages from people unknown and so uncouth. Do I have any say in this! After visiting my parents yesterday, I came home to such a long message from one such uncouth fellow close to Sheena. She is a nice lady, but my god. Sometimes I just wish life would deal me the hand of death and let me have peace. Life is just too hard at times. But that is my mind, days of negativity is rife.'

Her message showed her annoyance.

She removed 14 more men and women inclusive of that weird man and went on:

'One thing I forgot to say… For you, if you feel anyone here on my list is not worthy, I would delete him in a heartbeat, because for you my friend, I would do anything you ask.

Will you please smile now my friend KK?'

Some social media sites have their own sex appeal. I repeat my earlier averment.

But quite honestly, she was not looking for compliments on

her being slim which obviously she was not. By the way, we are all a tad overweight when we get older. Bad hormones. She sought to be forgiven for being blunt. She worked out. But found it quite absurd that any one human being or friend would tell another to slim down. She hastened to add, 'You yourself were not exactly the slim man you once were.' But she would never even dream of saying such a rude thing to anyone because she claimed she never tried not to stereotype her friends. Or justify how one should appear in a photo. She had ultimate faith in human beauty and found all human beings beautiful.

'I believe, my dear friend, you are rather jealous.' Ms Lehanga charged me.

But messaged me later:

'Then, there was this one Arron. He sent me a friend request last night. I accepted it going by the concept of mutual friends giving time to see if they are okay. This morning, another request came from same surname: Arron's wife. So this means she does not trust her own husband? Trust is installed here… What are women like? How pathetic it is not to trust…marriage, relationship or friendship. All these should be pure trust. That lady was so silly to follow her husband like that. But she would give her benefit of her doubt.

How strange women truly are—I hate this in women.'

She was chatting with me and then she asked, 'What is your feeling on some of the people on my list? I am contemplating, tell me? I admire you advice.'

Really in a quandary about what advice to give to her.

∽

Kudos to social media. You really have friends of all sorts with expectations of, equally, all sorts. About a minute ago this message came from Faiza Khan.

'Price of friendship. Sorry, the whole day I was very much busy with my office, family, my own life... because I'm the only earning member in my family. My father is a retired clerk in a department where there is no speed money; younger brother and sister are busy pursuing their studies. Please do solve this problem for me. Can you find a good boy for me for marriage? There's nobody to take my responsibility. I'm alone in my working place. I live in my office area without my family. You are most welcome, any time, if you are a bachelor or even a divorced man.'

Are these people crazy? Why would someone ask this of me? Do they think I look like a matchmaker? Delinquents. I swear they have sawdust where there should be brain cells...

One day, quite unexpectedly, I got this in my spam:

In honour of my friend: 'The Philosopher of Poetry'

Each stroke of ink flows down
To pen deep thoughts,
As he ponders everlasting truths
And afflictions from within his soul
Rough sketches of our world.

Then—'So dismal without you.'
There are people who feel dismal without me. I confess it to Professor Yadav.
'You are a sadist then,' Professor Yadav hushed.

'Well-aroused, tormenting.' This is the title of the review of my second book of poetry *An Armless Hand Writes* in *The Little*

Magazine. That was okay. The aftermath was more compelling. And then, there was an opinion:

'That is a very spontaneous and intriguing comment about the title of your book, very sexy, indeed, congrats... It's the kind of thing a lady would love to hear once in a lifetime from a man, "Well-aroused, and tormenting". Someone with an artful and daring mind has actually seen your title's uniqueness.' Ms Lehanga expressed herself, did not demur.

A few minutes go past and then, 'KKS, are you still keen? Check the list of cute singles that match with you,' said a mail in my inbox. 'All of them waiting for your response.' Then follow about twenty photographs of women aging from 45 to 55 with small, cryptic messages. Unreadable. I am married for twenty-seven years now. A recent photograph of me with my wife kept on the side table reminds me of it.

⁂

I asked how I could help her with her issues.

'Fold me inside of your heart and let me in...That's how,' Ms Lehanga replied.

Then followed a message:
Melodious bow,
Smoothly play your symphony,
Enthral my heart.
What do you think of this Haiku I wrote?'

It is the violin and the bow... I thought of this but did not convey it to her.

⁂

Models of possibility appear in various forms of social media. It is a means to escape a world where one gets appalled at the absence of privileges: privileges of looking at things, reading things like the ones aforementioned and hearing voices that may be alienated. Sometimes assertions seem like private confidences of estranged persons. Social media is only a reflection on the digital mirror of the world we live in. We come across the same kind of people in social media that we see in the real world. But, is it safe to say they appear in social media with a veneer on their faces? This veneer brings with it anonymity; a freedom to say things, a few examples of which I have given before, which in real life is almost well-nigh impossible to express. So you have persons like Ms Sheena offering kisses and Ms Lehanga seeking views on deletions/additions as if I am her approving authority. It is a mirror replete with banalities, frivolities and moral aberrations. Fortunately, there is no dearth of intellectual discourse on social media benefiting those keen in such discourses. A question lurks. One cannot imagine where and in which direction social media will go but one should be willing to wait and see.

EPILOGUE

Time to Say Adieu

I am conscious of the fact that writing is a job which does not yearn for glamour, and self-indulgence should never dictate the way to start writing, but, at times, it is agonizingly close and therefore difficult to ignore. Eidetic merger of insights and intuitions is at the core of my narratives. Preparing to ride a bicycle has never guided that merger. I have truly ridden the bicycle. I know both: the bicycle and the ride. I am equally comfortable with both. My perception has not been principally an act but a background against which all acts and behaviours stand out. In this book, I have looked at perception as an active process allowing it to winnow latent meanings from human action. On days I wrote, I felt like walking the road, the way I imagine I would, on the day of my death. Like moments just before death, which bring all memories of a man's life to him before he forgets everything for good, the end of the days I would write on would bring the same feelings to me.

For the sake of argument, let us say this book is as absurd and as weird as its writer. 'What shall I do with this absurdity?' the Yeatsean muse rings in my ears. The most important work a piece of writing performs is this: it helps the writer get out there what he thinks is essential. That's it. Much much later, I will be calling upon myself to judge where I stand. But that would be a task earmarked for a distant time. For the present, the price that I have to pay is the price of getting pushed into greater isolation which is an enlightened freedom—the freedom which illuminates the world inside me. Many writers aim for it. Few achieve it.